FROM BUSINESS STRATEGY TO INFORMATION TECHNOLOGY ROADMAP

A Practical Guide for Executives and Board Members

FROM BUSINESS STRATEGY TO INFORMATION TECHNOLOGY ROADMAP

A Practical Guide for Executives and Board Members

Tiffany Pham,
MBA, Harvard Business School

David K. Pham and Andrew T. Pham,
Authors of *Business-Driven IT-Wide Agile (Scrum) and Kanban (Lean) Implementation*

Forewords by:

Mitchell Fox
CEO, WGA Global Marketing, Former Group President, Condé Nast Publications

Dr. Larry Rothstein
Co-Chairman of the Board, No Limits Media, Former Editor, *Harvard Business Review*

Michael Weiner
Strategy Consultant, Revenue Storm, Former Vice President, EDS

Emily Simoness
Founder & Executive Director, Space on Ryder Farm

Kiran Rijhsinghani
Chairwoman, NYC Ballet Business& Professional Committee
Vice President, Weiss Multi Strategy Advisers

CRC Press
Taylor & Francis Group
Boca Raton   London   New York

CRC Press is an imprint of the
Taylor & Francis Group, an **informa** business

A PRODUCTIVITY PRESS BOOK

CRC Press
Taylor & Francis Group
6000 Broken Sound Parkway NW, Suite 300
Boca Raton, FL 33487-2742

© 2013 by Taylor & Francis Group, LLC
CRC Press is an imprint of Taylor & Francis Group, an Informa business

No claim to original U.S. Government works

Printed on acid-free paper
Version Date: 20121214

International Standard Book Number: 978-1-4665-8502-7 (Hardback)

Library of Congress Cataloging-in-Publication Data

Pham, Tiffany.
   From business strategy to information technology roadmap : a practical guide for executives and board members / Tiffany Pham, David K. Pham, and Andrew Pham.
      pages cm
   Includes bibliographical references and index.
   ISBN 978-1-4665-8502-7
   1. Information technology--Management. 2. Strategic planning. I. Pham, David Khoi. II. Pham, Andrew Thu. III. Title.

HD30.2.P489 2013
658.4'012--dc23   2012047654

Visit the Taylor & Francis Web site at
http://www.taylorandfrancis.com

and the CRC Press Web site at
http://www.crcpress.com

To Jessica and Kym with love

Contents

SECTION II AN INTRODUCTION TO LEAN, LEAN AND AGILE ORGANIZATION, AND LEAN AND AGILE IT

Praise for *From Business Strategy to Information Technology Roadmap*

From all that I have observed throughout the years, whether as President and CEO of companies or as an industry observer, I know you can only ignore the suggestions of Pham's book ... at your own peril. And it's a heck of a lot less money than getting this same advice from an expensive team of traditional consultants; it's faster and easy to implement the ideas in this book; and it will help your company to work more collaboratively and become more innovative.

Mitchell Fox
CEO, WGA Global Marketing
Former Group President, Condé Nast Publications

As Co-Chairman of the Board of No Limits Media ... and as a former Editor of the *Harvard Business Review*, I had the great pleasure of reading Tiffany Pham's book *From Business Strategy to Information Technology Roadmap*. The book makes a powerful case for the importance of any organization, profit-driven or nonprofit, to deeply connect its strategic thinking with its IT architecture and structure. Pham and her co-authors eloquently lay out their argument in a clear, step-by-step approach that guides the reader through the basics.

Larry Rothstein, PhD
Co-Chairman of the Board, No Limits Media
Former Editor, *Harvard Business Review*

I have very much enjoyed reading this new book and found it very realistic with a very logical and practical approach for how to create the necessary alignment between the business and IT organization. In our competitive world where IT can either be a strategic business enabler for competitive agility and advantage or a hindrance to the same, this book provides an easy to understand, yet profound, approach senior management can readily use. I recommend it to all senior management staff, both business and IT, and believe it should be considered as required reading in MBA programs.

Michael Weiner
Strategy Consultant, Revenue Storm
Former Vice President, EDS

What's remarkable about Pham's book is that it offers a detailed and systematic approach that feels completely intuitive. As such, one can learn from the very practical advice here, while preserving those all-important, if nebulous, instincts. *From Business Strategy to Information Technology Roadmap* feels especially useful because it understands deeply something paramount to artistry: collaboration. … In this book, Pham gets to the heart of both business strategy and IT, such that those with a strategy background can better understand the IT perspective and vice versa. She also provides an efficient, yet comprehensive, primer for the young entrepreneur trying to get a handle on what strategy looks like and how it interfaces with every part of the business. Reading this book at the genesis of my organization would have saved me a lot of time and headaches.

Emily Simoness
Founder and Executive Director, SPACE on Ryder Farm

My volunteer work, coupled with my full-time job on Wall Street, has shown me how organizational goals are helped or hindered by the quality of IT. With *From Business Strategy to Information Technology Roadmap*, I learned that Pham demonstrates the same interest in these two perspectives—from inside both the commercial enterprise and the nonprofit organization. In this very timely book, Pham and her co-authors lay out a concise, logical, and clear pathway that both business executives and IT leaders can use to intelligently derive an IT roadmap from the organization's business strategy as well as integrate IT into the fabric of the organization, providing innovative, creative solutions to enhance business operations.

Kiran Rijhsinghani
Chairwoman, New York City Ballet Business & Professional Committee
Vice President, Weiss Multi Strategy Advisers

Faced with much uncertainty and economic challenges, businesses today need to be flexible and able to adapt to changing strategies and federal regulations. IT system design is a reason I hear all too often regarding why we can't implement a new creative idea, whether it's due to cost or archaic systems. Looking into the future, this cannot be the excuse anymore; companies need to consider IT design as a top priority and interlace it with their business strategy. This book gives a simple, systematic approach to technology design and business strategy—a must read to understand how to compete in the ever-changing global landscape. It emphasizes the need for business and tech minds to come together to develop optimal solutions, challenging the historic IT stereotype of acting like a silo and resisting large change. *From Business Strategy to Information Technology Roadmap* presents a simplified approach to moving your enterprise toward success and developing a long-term sustainable strategy and IT foundation.

Stephanie Bartz
Director of Strategic Planning, United Healthcare

What I like about Pham's book is that it is easy to read with real examples of business case and business strategy. Likewise, I also like the overall organization of the book, which is very logical and easy to follow. I personally recommend this book to any IT executives who would like—or need—to build an IT or technology roadmap that can more clearly support his or her company's or nonprofit association's business strategy.

Adam Warner
IT Management, Education Service Center, Region 10

About the Authors

Tiffany Pham graduated with a BA in Economics and International Studies, with Distinction, from Yale University and an MBA from Harvard Business School.

Prior to Harvard Business School, Tiffany Pham was in M&A Investment Banking on Wall Street and has since worked on strategic initiatives at multi-billion dollar media conglomerates. In addition to this, she also serves on the Board of Trustees for Provincetown Film Society, the Board of Directors for No Limits Media, the Board of Advisors for Space on Ryder Farm, and the Business Committee for the New York City Ballet.

Tiffany Pham can be contacted at: TiffanyPham@aya.yale.edu.

David Pham, a prolific software creator, is the co-author of the book *Business-Driven IT-Wide Agile (Scrum) and Kanban (Lean) Implementation*, also by Productivity Press.

In addition to this, David Pham is also a Sun-certified Java and Microsoft-certified developer. A technology entrepreneur, he has held top positions with a number of start-ups, first as Chief Technology Officer (CTO) with KTD Media Corporation based in New York and then as President of a Web-based company based in Rhode Island.

While not working, David Pham enjoys spending time with his family as well as sharing his ideas with others. To this effect, he was the invited keynote speaker at the DevChatt Conference for software developers in Nashville, Tennessee, in 2011.

Andrew Pham, an IEEE senior member, PMP, and PMI-ACP, is the co-author with David Pham of *Business-Driven IT-Wide Agile (Scrum) and Lean (Kanban) Implementation*.

A seasoned IT professional and executive coach, Andrew Pham has trained hundreds of business and software professionals throughout the world in Agile (Scrum) and Lean (Kanban).

Prior to taking on coaching as one of his main activities, Andrew Pham had held several senior positions in IT management, enterprise architecture, system integration, software development, and project management within many organizations of different types and sizes.

Acknowledgments

We are greatly appreciative of the people who helped us with the writing of this book.

First and foremost, we would like to thank our family. Their unwavering and unconditional love and support made this all possible.

Next, we would like to thank the people whose suggestions and ideas have helped us further improve the book; in particular, Stephanie Bartz (United Healthcare), Jameelah Calhoun (American Express), Scott DeBenedett (Lightyear Capital), Diane Shao (Harvard Medical School), and Adam Warner (Education Service Center, Region 10).

Likewise, we would like to thank Mitchell Fox (CEO of WGA Global Marketing and former Group President of Condé Nast Publications), Larry Rothstein (Co-Chairman of the Board at No Limits Media and a former Editor of the *Harvard Business Review*), Michael Weiner (Strategy Consultant at Revenue Storm), Emily Simoness (Founder and Executive Director of Space on Ryder Farm), and Kiran Rijhsinghani (Vice President at Weiss Multi Strategy Advisers and Chairwoman of the New York City Ballet Business & Professional Committee) for having reviewed our book during its early stages and written such thoughtful forewords.

Additionally, we would like to thank the team at Productivity Press for their dedication to our book: Kristine Mednansky, acquiring editor; Randy Burling, project editor; Laurie Schlags, project coordinator; and Karen Schober, editorial assistant.

Last but not least, we would like to thank all of the authors whose works are cited within the following pages. To those we have not mentioned, please know that we have made every effort to trace all ideas and copyright holders. However, if any of these have inadvertently been overlooked, please let our publisher or us know so that we can make the necessary amendments at the earliest opportunity.

What Is This Book About?

The goal of this book is to guide executives and board members through the process of formalizing a strong and sustainable business strategy and then using that to drive the creation of an IT (information technology) roadmap that will help make their business strategy happen. As we mentioned in the Preface, this process can be applied to companies of all types, whether in the for-profit or nonprofit sector, and all sizes, ranging from start-up to very large.

To this effect, there are 12 chapters (plus 2 case studies and 7 appendices) in the book, where you will find the following topics covered in what we believe to be sufficient detail. We hope this will enable you to put your newfound knowledge immediately into action.

Section I: A Concise Introduction to Business Strategy: Concepts and Formulation

Chapter 1: From Mission, Vision, and Values to Business Model
The goal of this chapter is to introduce you to several strategic concepts that will be useful for further discussion on business strategy. We will discuss elements related to mission, vision, and values, which are used to formulate the strategy of either a commercial company or nonprofit association. We will additionally speak about the different aspects of a business model, which also can serve as the foundation of an organization's business strategy.

Chapter 2: Business Strategy and Its Formulation
The goal of this chapter is to walk you in greater detail through the various techniques used to formalize a business strategy. In writing this chapter, we hope it will prove particularly helpful to IT leaders who are otherwise unfamiliar with these business concepts. For business leaders, we hope it will serve as a useful refresher and, in any case, a bridge between the two sides in light of the discussion on business strategy and IT alignment that follows.

Section II: An Introduction to Lean, Lean and Agile Organization, and Lean and Agile IT

Chapter 3: What Do We Mean by Lean, Lean and Agile Organization, and Lean and Agile IT?

As fervent proponents of a new generation of Lean (and, therefore, Agile) businesses and Lean and Agile IT for customer value creation and innovation, we have written this chapter to serve as an introduction to the concepts of Lean (and, therefore, Agile) as well as their application to business and IT. A comprehensive discussion of these concepts will provide you with a solid foundation for understanding what is required for a business and IT organization to be Lean and Agile and be more customer value driven and innovative.

Section III: From Business Strategy to IT Roadmap: An Introduction to Enterprise Architecture (EA)

Chapter 4: An Introduction to Business Strategy and IT Alignment

The goal of this chapter is to review some of the reasons why IT is frequently not well aligned with a company's business strategy. Such a misalignment oftentimes results from the fact that IT is often inclined to serve the executives who have the most clout or largest budget—regardless of the organization's overall strategy. As such, we will show why such a situation is wasteful of the organization's resources and ultimately untenable. By the end of the chapter, we will then introduce the reader to the concept of enterprise architecture (EA), which we will use to apply a solution toward the lack of understanding between business and IT and close this gap on misalignment.

Chapter 5: More on Enterprise Architecture

Having briefly presented the concept of EA in Chapter 4, the goal of this chapter is to lead you into a deeper discussion about the EA and its different layers. This chapter introduces the EA's four main layers: enterprise business architecture, enterprise IT application architecture, enterprise IT data architecture, and finally, enterprise IT infrastructure architecture. Given the importance of the Internet and its potential threat to enterprise security, we also will discuss the emerging layer that is becoming known as the enterprise IT security architecture, which we believe will take on a more important role in the EA.

Section IV: From Business Strategy to an Agile and Lean IT Roadmap: The Formulation Process

Chapter 6: A High-Level Overview of the IT Roadmap Formulation Process

The goal of this chapter is to provide a high-level overview of the four steps required to develop an IT roadmap, including: (1) an assessment of the current business and IT situation, (2) an identification of the future business and IT needs, (3) the identification of the business and IT gaps, and finally, (4) the creation of the IT roadmap that will best support the organization's business strategy.

Chapter 7: More on the IT Roadmap Formulation Process
Our main objective here is to walk you in detail through the four-step formulation process of an IT roadmap. The first two steps provide details on how to identify and review different artifacts related to the current and future business and IT situation. We then walk the reader through the details of how to review the organization's needs in IT strategic and operational alignment and discuss how to identify gaps between current IT and future IT needs. Lastly, this chapter details the process of deriving the IT roadmap from the aforementioned gaps while providing a complete picture of the different components an IT roadmap should contain.

Chapter 8: From a Business Unit's IT Roadmap to an Enterprise IT Roadmap
In the case that you first create an IT roadmap for only one business unit, we show you how to translate this into an enterprise-wide IT roadmap.

Chapter 9: IT and Mergers and Acquisitions (M&A) Activities
With IT often considered a mere afterthought when it comes to mergers and acquisitions (M&A), it is our intent here to change that mindset and suggest to business executives that they integrate IT very early on in both their thinking and planning for M&A. The foremost reason for this suggestion is that we have seen many M&A processes otherwise become delayed, fail to take shape, or cost more than they should. The other reason for this suggestion is that we believe that having a better assessment of the successful integration of two organizations' IT could—and should—have a significant impact on the valuation of the overall M&A process.

Chapter 10: Change Management
The goal of this chapter is to introduce you to the importance of setting up a plan that will help you manage the changes that come with the creation and execution of a business strategy and IT roadmap. This plan should enable you to both mobilize the troops and ease their concerns as your organization transitions into the future.

Section V: From IT Roadmap Formulation to Execution

Chapter 11: Strategy Is Execution
The goal of this chapter is to discuss the actual implementation of an IT roadmap, highlighting significant facets, such as the organization of a Business and IT Governance Board or IT Steering Committee, the regular review of work progress and budget variance, and the review of business goals. By assessing these key elements, you will be able to better gauge the IT roadmap's real progress and true contribution to the organization's value creation and innovation.

Chapter 12: Parting Thoughts
This chapter offers key takeaways from the book, outlining some lessons for successfully developing a business strategy-driven IT roadmap.

Section VI: Case Studies

Case Study 1: Commercial Case Study: All About HatWare
This case study shows how All About HatWare, a commercial family business, used our approach to formulate its business strategy and create a new IT roadmap, ultimately turning the struggling family business into a successful multimillion-dollar business.

Case Study 2: Nonprofit Case Study: US Against Illiteracy
This case study shows how US Against Illiteracy, a nonprofit organization based in New York City, used our approach to build its IT roadmap to better serve the association's new business strategy and social mission.

Appendices

A: The 10 Questions an IT Leader Should Ask His or Her CEO or Board Members
B: The 10 Questions the CEO or Board Member Should Ask His or Her IT Leader
C: Leveraging Social Media for Business Strategy
D: Leveraging Mobile Technology for Business Strategy
E: Leveraging Cloud Computing for Business Strategy
F: The Business Case for a New Business Technology Project
G: Buy or Build (Commercial Off-the-Shelf Package Implementation or In-House Software Development)?

Who Should Read This Book?

The intended audience for this book is C-level executives (CEO, COO, CFO, CMO, CIO, CTO, CDO, etc.) and their senior staffs as well as board members. The concepts and processes highlighted in this book are intended to help facilitate better dialogue among these top executives, enabling them to work together to formalize their business strategy and develop an IT roadmap that will help make this business strategy happen.

Preface

Welcome to *From Business Strategy to Information Technology Roadmap: A Practical Guide for Executives and Board Members*. Whether you are a CEO, CFO, board member, or an IT executive, this book is for you. As you work with your team to clarify your business strategy and create an IT roadmap, this book will guide you forward by providing you with a straightforward process along with many examples to follow and from which to draw inspiration.

Unlike some other books, you will not find theories or grandiose ideas in this book. To the contrary, this book has been written for business executives and technology leaders with only the intent to help solve the real-world problems these professionals face in their daily responsibilities, either to further grow their business or get it out of dangerous zones amid today's tough competition.

As you read on, you also will realize that the book has been written for executives in both the commercial and nonprofit sectors. This explains why you will find that there are two case studies at the end of the book: one is about a commercial family business, which thrived to become a multi-million dollar company, and the other is about a nonprofit association, which fights against child illiteracy based in New York City.

To represent the diversity of the book's audience and convey their different perspectives, you will find five forewords written by executive leaders from both the commercial and nonprofit sectors:

1. **Mitchell Fox**
   CEO, WGA Global Marketing
   Former Group President, Condé Nast Publications
2. **Larry Rothstein, PhD**
   Co-Chairman of the Board, No Limits Media
   Former Editor, *Harvard Business Review*
3. **Michael Weiner**
   Strategy Consultant, Revenue Storm
   Former Vice President, EDS

4. **Emily Simoness**
   Founder and Executive Director, Space on Ryder Farm
5. **Kiran Rijhsinghani**
   Chairwoman, New York City Ballet Business & Professional Committee
   Vice President, Weiss Multi Strategy Advisers

As IT has become omnipresent, we consider it critical that organizations of all types and sizes know how to leverage this marvelous tool to bring about more innovation and value to their customers or constituents.

It has been a true pleasure to formalize and bring our experiences and knowledge to you. We hope that you will enjoy reading the book as much as we have enjoyed writing it.

Tiffany Pham
David Pham
Andrew Pham

Foreword by Mitchell Fox

It's not unusual for companies to have functional silos imbedded into their culture; sometimes dysfunctional silos.

The sales organization doesn't work well with research or product development, and finance is usually everyone's sworn enemy as budgets are examined and questioned and of late reduced. Marketing departments often resent sales, and say they need more from finance to be effective.

Then, there is IT. Often no one understands them, not sure of what they do, and certainly know less about how they do it. Seemingly, their budgets never get cut, and they have free reign to hire and expand their departments, often in reality or perception at the expense of all other departments.

They love detail. They love to tell you how the clock works, when all you want to know is what time it is. This is simply a fundamental disconnect.

This is not abstract—this is reality, from what I have seen managing diverse companies such as Condé Nast, to mention a few.

Is it sustainable?

No.

For companies of a certain size (larger, more likely) to be competitive on a global scale, they have to work in an interdisciplinary construct. They have to be able to work across disciplines, departments, and layers of management. You see it all the time in younger company staff who simply do not know any better. In a very organic way, they have created organizational structures that permit the company to act and react to market conditions with whatever (often limited) resources they have—whether it be from one department or another, from a seasoned veteran or from a new young, inexperienced employee. No matter … success is the goal, and achieving it with whatever assets the company has to bring to bear against a challenge is only a good thing.

Not so always for larger companies with long legacies of functional/dysfunctional silos. This is why Eric Schmidt of Google constantly reminds us that innovation comes from younger companies, not established ones, because operationally established companies cannot, and do not, have the institutional aptitude to "think different." (Thank you, Apple.) They cannot change their own self-perception; they cannot change the ways they do things or the ways they interact with each other, to see a new opportunity, a new market, or simply a new and more efficient way to operate.

Now, here comes a roadmap from Tiffany Pham and her co-authors in a text that offers two practical examples on collaboration between the business executive suite and the technology folks in their companies.

I happen to know Tiffany Pham personally, as a friend and colleague, and I've heard Ms. Pham describe her thinking on a number of subjects. I know she is a champion of collaboration, of working together, especially between business executives and technologists, and how doing so restores a company's focus on possibilities and opportunities.

It's easy to see why her book has so much value, especially to those who need it most (larger companies, with long legacies, change averse), and I hope business executives of those kinds of companies will read it and will have their senior management and technology staffs read it. However, if it becomes a book for the converted (smaller, more nimble innovative growing companies), then it will accelerate their ability to capture market share, and, in hindsight, this might be just another touchstone moment for certain industries. It happened when the film and radio industries couldn't see television coming, when the television networks couldn't understand cable, and when all these companies couldn't understand the Internet.

They just couldn't "think different." So, each successive iteration of media was created by a group of young companies, who really didn't know the "rules" (functional silos, territorial managers, etc.). They just pursued success—collectively.

With all of the intellectual capital imbedded in large companies; a deep (and long) recession on our hands; global markets being challenged by economic and currency woes; natural resources becoming more and more scarce, expensive, and in many cases, politically volatile, from oil-based products to coal-based factories, it's hard to believe that any company would ignore the sage advice to collaborate across disciplines. And if you agree that technology will drive everything (!), then start with the technologists in the company, get them together with the executive management groups, start from the top, lead from the front, and then it will trickle down to become culturally imbedded.

From all that I have observed throughout the years, whether as President and CEO of companies or as an industry observer, I know you can only ignore the suggestions of Pham's book … at your own peril. And it's a heck of a lot less money than getting this same advice from an expensive team of traditional consultants; it's faster and easy to implement the ideas in this book; and it will help your company to work more collaboratively and become more innovative, with creative technology solutions that come as a direct result of your technology and executive team's collective business strategies and vision.

I have enjoyed reading and learning from this book, and I know you will as well. Go forth and good reading.

Mitchell Fox
CEO, WGA Global Marketing
Former Group President, Condé Nast Publications

Foreword by
Larry Rothstein

As Co-Chairman of the Board of No Limits Media, a Boston-based nonprofit organization whose mission is to change the image of people with disabilities, and as a former Editor of the *Harvard Business Review*, I had the great pleasure of reading Tiffany Pham's book *From Business Strategy to Information Technology Roadmap*. The book makes a powerful case for the importance of any organization, profit-driven or nonprofit, to deeply connect its strategic thinking with its IT architecture and structure. Pham and her co-authors eloquently lay out their argument in a clear, step-by-step approach that guides the reader through the basics—from strategic thinking, citing such foundational writers as Michael Porter, to developing realistic financial goals and business processes while concurrently leveraging Lean and Agile concepts. The authors then proceed to explain developments in IT architecture and infrastructure while also providing a simple process for the reader to follow and use to create an IT roadmap, informing and elucidating in a highly concise and effective manner. Finally, they show how both business strategy and IT architecture and infrastructure can work together to enhance any organization's capability to thrive.

Through the use of two in-depth cases studies, the authors bring home the book's lessons in great detail. As someone in the nonprofit world, I paid particular attention to the case study of nonprofit US Against Illiteracy (USAI), whose goal is to dramatically increase revenue via new technology-supported processes while promoting books written by the very children it serves. After analyzing the organization's mission, team structure, and current business processes and IT applications, the authors skillfully illustrate how USAI's IT architecture, infrastructure, and internal operations were highly inefficient, diverting precious resources away from its mission. The authors then demonstrate how USAI could effectively turn things around by leveraging creative business processes and solutions as well as innovative IT. I particularly appreciated the discussion around USAI's launch of new products and its creative use of social media and mobile technology to achieve the deep social and business impact the organization aims to make on the lives of children, as well as to ensure its financial viability, even as a nonprofit organization.

Too often, in my experience, nonprofit organizations are unaware of the lessons that can be gained from the profit-driven business and technology worlds. In this invaluable book, the authors have designed a splendid guide to coupling strategic thinking with IT architecture and infrastructure, teaching lessons that will be invaluable and long lasting to No Limits Media, executives, managers, and other decision makers. Indeed, they convey the numerous opportunities the reader has to increase profitability, improve efficiency, and make a greater impact on the world using formidable technology tools that are well-aligned with the organization's business strategy.

Not only has it been a tremendous pleasure for me to read and write a foreword for *From Business Strategy to Information Technology Roadmap: A Practical Guide for Executives and Board Members*, but I am also glad that I now have this book to refer to in my toolbox as I lead the No Limits Media board to develop new strategies that support our mission, vision, and goals and discuss how to innovatively and efficiently leverage modern technology to make our business plans a reality.

Larry Rothstein, PhD
Co-Chairman of the Board, No Limits Media
Former Editor, Harvard Business Review

Foreword by Michael Weiner

As a former vice president at EDS (Electronic Data Systems), headquartered in Plano, TX, and over the past 20 years as a business strategist/consultant, I have been traveling the world (from the United States to India to China) to help companies of all sizes accomplish growth, profitability, and competitive advantage by aligning and leveraging their IT capabilities and organizations. During this period, enormous competitive, technological, and economic changes have caused my customers' executive teams to be highly challenged to develop the necessary business agility to change as fast as their market required.

My experience is that the most successful companies I have worked with learned to use their IT organization and CIO (chief information officer) as strategic weapons, trying to align the IT function with their constantly changing strategies and agendas. Successful industry leaders and fast-growing companies alike learn to use technology in constantly new ways to incrementally, as well as strategically, enhance their enterprise order to cash processes, deliver new sources of differentiated value, and connect to customers in ways that make their customers more successful. They see a new era for the need for even more information agility.

However, for the majority of companies, this is not the story. Instead, most companies find their IT to be ineffective, poorly aligned to their business, and unresponsive, with low return on investment (ROI) and low customer value. This situation becomes more frustrating over time and leads to a spiral of functional disagreements, mistrust, and lack of the needed IT leverage in an economy that is becoming more, not less, IT-intensive then ever before.

Why the difference between industry leaders and the rest of their industry? The answer is not simple. However, the authors of this remarkable book do a great job of identifying for all business and IT leaders in a very simple, straightforward way how to build more powerful, practical approaches to developing winning business strategies that align and integrate IT as a strategic enabler to accelerate enterprise leanness, agility, and market success.

The book quickly takes the reader from concepts to frameworks, with a very practical approach and tools, based on Agile and Lean, as well as on the concept of enterprise architecture. It quickly becomes obvious that the book offers a new easy-to-understand model for executive teams to follow in their effort to create more business agility and a Lean organization, while developing innovative solutions that will allow more market differentiation and also will bring in more customer value.

My hope for each reader is that *From Business Strategy to Information Technology Roadmap: A Practical Guide for Executives and Board Members*, which can be read in just a couple of hours, can provide the impetus to share ideas with one another at an upcoming executive staff meeting with an opportunity to grow both their company and career.

I have very much enjoyed reading this book and found it very realistic with a very logical and practical approach for how to create the necessary alignment between the business and IT organization.

In our competitive world where IT can either be a strategic business enabler for competitive agility and advantage or a hindrance to the same, this book provides an easy to understand, yet profound, approach senior management can readily use. I recommend it to all senior management staff, both business and IT, and believe it should be considered as required reading in MBA programs.

Michael Weiner
Strategy Consultant, Revenue Storm
Former Vice President, EDS

Foreword by Emily Simoness

I had never planned to be an executive director of a nonprofit. I was working in New York City and saw a community that articulated a need for a creative workspace. Three years later, I find myself running SPACE on Ryder Farm, an artist residency program housed on a working organic farm in Brewster, New York. Despite my apparent lack of preparation for the role, in its first two seasons, SPACE has hosted over 200 artists; among these were Tony winners, Obie winners, and Pulitzer Prize finalists. While I may not have known it at the time, the ideas expressed in *From Business Strategy to Information Technology Roadmap: A Practical Guide for Executives and Board Members* have been instrumental in the success of my organization.

In the early days of SPACE, I made a lot of decisions based on instinct. Like a lot of entrepreneurs or start-up leaders, I trusted my gut more than anything else. Sure, there was plenty of strategic planning, but when push came to shove, intuition ruled the day. Those early days feel so precarious that anything that violated my visceral impulse of what was right for the organization (no matter how much sense it made on paper) seemed out of bounds. What's remarkable about Pham's book is that it offers a detailed and systematic approach that feels completely intuitive. As such, one can learn from the very practical advice here, while preserving those all-important, if nebulous, instincts.

From Business Strategy to Information Technology Roadmap feels especially useful because it understands deeply something paramount to artistry: collaboration. Successful institutional development is all about collaboration, and successful collaboration (as we have learned in the arts) is about truly understanding where the other party is coming from. To empathize deeply with the other party's values, goals, needs, and experiences is the essential first step to understanding how to best create together. In this book, Pham gets to the heart of both business strategy and IT, such that those with a strategy background can better understand the IT perspective and vice versa. She also provides an efficient, yet comprehensive, primer for the young entrepreneur trying to get a handle on what strategy looks like and how it interfaces with every part of the business. Reading this book at the genesis of my organization would have saved me a lot of time and headaches.

Over the past three years, Pham has served as a key advisor for SPACE on Ryder Farm. Without her advice, business savvy, and support, SPACE would not be where it is today. Structured, yet intuitive, systematic while still organic, *From Business Strategy to Information Technology Roadmap* is a natural companion for anyone looking to better integrate their business strategy and IT, and a useful conversation starter for any institution seriously interested in the executive team's collaboration.

What a gift for us that Pham has so readily codified her advice into a very practical book, not only useful to self-made leaders like myself, but also to graduate students from both business and technology schools.

It has been a pleasure and an honor for me to review Pham's book. I am glad that I have read it, learned from it, and now have it in my library for my team's and my ongoing reference.

Emily Simoness
Founder and Executive Director, SPACE on Ryder Farm

Foreword by
Kiran Rijhsinghani

As the Chairwoman of New York City Ballet's Business & Professional Committee, I have had the opportunity to work with Tiffany Pham to help New York City Ballet engage with New York City's community of young professionals. In that capacity, I have come to admire Pham's work ethic, intelligence, and commitment to excellence. A graduate of Yale and Harvard Business School, she has used her enormous talents to make significant contributions to the work of our committee.

My volunteer work, coupled with my full-time job on Wall Street, has shown me how organizational goals are helped or hindered by the quality of IT. With *From Business Strategy to Information Technology Roadmap: A Practical Guide for Executives and Board Members*, I learned that Pham demonstrates the same interest in these two perspectives—from inside both the commercial enterprise and the nonprofit organization. In this very timely book, Pham and her co-authors lay out a concise, logical, and clear pathway that both business executives and IT leaders can use to intelligently derive an IT roadmap from the organization's business strategy as well as integrate IT into the fabric of the organization, providing innovative, creative solutions to enhance business operations.

While the discussion on well-respected research such as Porter's Five Forces takes the dialogue of organizational strategy to a new level, Pham and her co-authors delightfully surprise us by pointing out that Porter's value chain model may have made IT a supporting activity rather than a primary activity, as it should now become with the arrival of and disruption by social networks and mobile technology. Thus, Pham and her co-authors persuade us, with great conviction, that in crafting an organizational strategy, IT should not be an afterthought, but instead serve as a contributing and decisive force at inception.

In my experience as a professional on Wall Street and a volunteer within a nonprofit organization, I spend a lot of time thinking about the most effective ways to further the goals of the organizations that I serve. To that end, I read a lot of books, and I take pains to observe what works and what does not work in real business and in society at large. This book provides a holistic and renewed view of organizations in a way that I have rarely seen, and gives the role of IT its rightful place in today's world—revolutionized by Apple, Twitter, and Facebook, to name a few. This book has provided me with many ideas and tools that I can use in my volunteer and for-profit work, and I believe any business and IT leader would benefit from reading it. Pham's passion for business and technology is obvious; her ability to apply sound academic research to solve real-world problems is undeniable; and last but not least, her communication style is clear and concise.

Having now known and worked with Pham for many years on the New York City Ballet's Business & Professional Committee, I am so happy that she decided to write this book to share her passion and thoughts beyond those of us lucky enough to work with her personally.

Kiran Rijhsinghani
Chairwoman, New York City Ballet Business & Professional Committee
Vice President, Weiss Multi Strategy Advisers

A CONCISE INTRODUCTION TO BUSINESS STRATEGY: CONCEPTS AND FORMULATION

Business strategy has long been a popular topic of discussion. As a result, there are hundreds, if not thousands, of books and articles that deal with the subject.

This said, we do not intend to ask you to continually refer to other books or articles for further information. Instead, we will provide a short introduction to business strategy, thereby setting the stage and providing a framework for the rest of our discussion in this book.

In the following pages, we will first review a few well-known business strategy concepts and frameworks, which we will then leverage, along with some new ideas and IT (information technology) concepts, to build an effective IT roadmap, whether for a commercial company or a nonprofit association.

Chapter 1

From Mission, Vision, and Values to Business Model

1.1 Chapter Objective

The goal of this chapter is to introduce you, the reader, to the concepts frequently used in business strategy formulation: mission, vision, and values. At the same time, we will also introduce you to the concept of a business model, which is also considered the foundation of an organization's business strategy.

1.2 Mission, Vision, and Values

1.2.1 Mission

What does your company have to offer to the world? The video rental service provider Blockbuster used to tout its mission of "bringing entertainment home." Meanwhile, BMW considers its mission to be "the world's leading provider of premium products and premium services for individual mobility." Facebook's mission, on the other hand, is "to create a more open and connected world."

As you construct such a mission statement for your organization, it is important to coherently articulate your organization's particular purpose for existing. Consider your organization's aims and desired impact on your customers or constituents. This mission statement will, after all, ultimately shape your organization's actions and guide your decisions going forward.

While defining your ogranization's mission is a first step, a mission statement alone is too abstract of a concept from which to derive a business strategy. Therefore, we must next explore a more specific, tangible concept before we can successfully create a business strategy: the concept of vision.

1.2.2 Vision

When we refer to an organization's vision, we are referring to how the CEO (Chief Executive Officer) and senior executive team envision the organization's future positioning over the years—which can be either right or wrong for the organization.

For example, IKEA's former CEO Anders Dahlvig reported in his book, *The IKEA Edge*, that the furniture company's unique and all-encompassing vision was to "create a better life for the majority of the people."[1] As it turned out, IKEA has detailed and implemented this vision quite successfully so far.

On the other hand, readers familiar with Blockbuster's history know that, until recently, Blockbuster's vision was to open stores as close as physically possible to its customers. As it turned out, that vision was ultimately the wrong guiding vision for Blockbuster's business strategy because competitors like Netflix took advantage of the explosive growth in online streaming and convenient rental by mail, capturing Blockbuster's remaining market share at the same time it faced competition from other brick-and-mortar retailers, such as Walmart or Target.

What the above implies is that it is critical for executives to have the right vision and strategy, something we will discuss in more detail in future chapters.

Going back to the need for the right vision, once it has been identified, the organization should try to translate it into financial goals, as much as possible. Doing this will provide teams with measurements that will help establish more specific expectations for their business strategy and action plan's performance. We will discuss this in further detail in Chapter 2.

1.2.3 Values

While providing a tangible vision is the next important step, asserting values (also called "behaviors" by former General Electric CEO Jack Welch in his book *Winning*[2]) is another critical component of business strategy. Dahlvig, for example, noted in his aforementioned book that IKEA's success relies on values based on the following behaviors: (1) simplicity, (2) delegating and accepting responsibility, (3) striving to meet reality, and (4) cost consciousness.

Why are values so important? It is because they are what ultimately distinguish one organization's business strategy from another's. Imagine that a pharmaceutical company wishes to differentiate itself from competitors, based on the trust it is building with customers. It may want to assert that one of its values is "to never to source an ingredient if there is a lack of visibility as to its origin, no matter how solid the relationship between the company and the ingredient's provider." Because this pharmaceutical company manufactures prescription medicine that must be used over the long-term, it stands to profit greatly if it continues to engender trust and increase sales to repeating customers.

Contrastingly, the lack of respect for such values crumbled the foundations of accounting firm Arthur Andersen's original mission to audit, displaying a lack of what Jack Welch calls "conscientiousness." This caused the company to ultimately collapse after it diverted into the consulting business, favoring a more aggressive and creative billing.

1.3 Business Model

In addition to the mission, vision, and values, there is another concept that can be used to determine an organization's business strategy: the business model. So what, exactly, is a business model?

Generally speaking, there is no single agreed-upon definition as to what a business model is. But inspired from Saul Kaplan, author of *The Business Model Innovation Factory*,[3] a business model should address the following:

- ■ How does an organization create values?
- ■ How does an organization deliver values?
- ■ How does an organization capture compensation for the values it creates?

At the same time, some other authors suggest that a business model is how an organization plans to make money. Therefore, a business model should define a commercial company's target customers or a nonprofit association's constituents, and assert how that organization intends to create value for those people. Still, other authors suggest that a business model should address how the organization plans to market and deliver its merchandise or service to its customers or constituents. More recently, a group of authors from Duke University has stated that a business model also should answer questions related to revenue mix, market share, and industry ranking.[4]

According again to Dahlvig, IKEA's business model defines most of the above criteria. As he wrote in his previously mentioned book, he considers IKEA's business model to be based on a desire to bring quality furniture to regular people and allow them the opportunity to view and pick up their merchandise themselves, conveniently bringing home this merchandise in flat-packed packages at consequently affordable prices.[1] As such, IKEA's business model directly addresses significant components of its business strategy, which we will discuss in further detail in Chapter 2.

1.4 Takeaways

Before you can create a business strategy, you need to identify the organization's mission, vision, and values. This will help, in turn, to differentiate the organization's business strategy from that of its competitors. Otherwise, developing an organization's business model also can be used to help define the organization's business strategy.

References

1. Dahlvig, A. 2012. *The IKEA edge: Building global growth and social good at the world's most iconic home store.* New York: McGraw-Hill, pp. 10, 58–62 .
2. Welch, J. 2005. *Winning.* New York: HarperBusiness, pp. 17–24.
3. Kaplan, S. 2012. *The business model innovation factory: How to stay relevant when the world is changing.* Hoboken, NJ: John Wiley & Sons.
4. Duke Corporation Education. 2012. *Translating strategy into action.* Chicago: Dearborn Trade Publishing, p. 88.

Chapter 2

Business Strategy and Its Formulation

2.1 Chapter Objective

This chapter introduces you to the specific concept of business strategy and its formulation, discussing aspects such as value creation and competitive analysis. Likewise, this chapter also introduces you to examples of financial projections that will provide more tangible expectations for a business strategy and ultimately help to drive the creation and execution of a well-aligned IT roadmap.

2.2 What Is Business Strategy?

How do you define a concept as abstract and undefined as "business strategy"? In simple language, a business strategy is a coordinated set of choices that positions an organization to generate superior long-term financial or social returns.

To be a good business strategy, an organization's business strategy must fulfill three criteria: internal consistency, external consistency, and dynamic consistency (Figure 2.1). As you read on, you will learn how to satisfy each of these key criteria.

2.2.1 Key Criteria for a Good Business Strategy

2.2.1.1 Internal Consistency

As you formulate a new business strategy, the set of choices you make should tie together so that the sum of the parts is greater than the whole. Each strategic decision should be carefully evaluated and tailored to deliver the unique value your

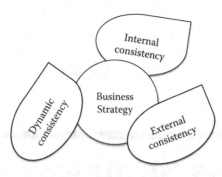

Figure 2.1 Key criteria for a good business strategy.

organization aims to offer its customers or constituents. If you fail to do this, you risk having your organization's activities not mesh in a compelling manner, thereby creating an unsustainable business strategy.

Therefore, it is important to begin the process of business strategy formulation by defining what value your organization will be delivering to its customers or constituents, otherwise known as your *value proposition*. Accordingly, a value proposition resolves three basic issues:

1. What needs will your organization serve?
2. Which customers or constituents your organization will serve?
3. What relative price, if applicable, will your organization charge?

Deciding what needs you should serve will probably be the first choice you face. If your organization has the unique ability to offer a product or service that fulfills a distinct need or subset of needs, then it may very well warrant your attention.

As you consider which customers or constituents you will serve, note that there are different ways to segment a population. While it might be suitable to base your customer or constituent segmentation on geography, demographics, or psychographics, it is clear that strong value propositions frequently target those who have previously been overlooked by other players in the industry or social sector.

In the case of a commercial company, when determining what relative price you will charge, it is important to consider whether or not your target customers have been over- or underserved by the industry. If customers have typically been overserved, then your value proposition may consist of streamlining costs, enabling you to adequately meet customer needs while offering, such as Walmart, a lower relative price. If customers have typically been underserved, then your value proposition may consist of enhancing the current offering, allowing you to offer a superior product, such as BMW, and charge a premium price.

As you forge your value proposition, keep in mind that in order to demonstrate internal consistency, the choices you make should properly reinforce each other, within the context of your organization's team, resources, or processes. This could mean that you may have to restructure some of them as Marissa Mayer, the new Yahoo! CEO, recently did in asking the company's teams to come back to the office to work, in support of her new vision and strategy.

2.2.1.2 External Consistency

A solid strategy will tap into opportunities that are consistent with external conditions. Therefore, it is important to examine what peripheral factors might positively impact your organization. For example, if the negotiating abilities of suppliers or partners are particularly weak within your industry, especially with regard to your organization's position, you may want to formulate a strategy that is consistent with this external aspect by basing your business strategy on leveraging the low costs from suppliers; this, in turn, would allow you to offer customers an exceptionally low price, as in Walmart's case.

A solid business strategy also should reduce threats presented by external conditions, taking into account the potentially negative effects of such factors as existing rivals, new entrants, substitutes, government regulation, and technological changes. As you forge a business strategy, it must align with the conditions of the outside world.

2.2.1.3 Dynamic Consistency

Most importantly, while a business strategy must be consistent with internal and external contexts, it also must demonstrate the robust ability to adapt to a changing and competitive environment; this applies for all organizations, even nonprofit associations. Demonstrating such dynamic consistency does not mean, though, that the organizations can radically implement changing strategies without adapting some of their core competencies, as we will see later on in Section 2.3.1.1. Instead, we are proponents of dynamic continuity, whereby your organization's core mission, vision, and value proposition remain the same, but the delivery of your value adapts to internal and external forces.

2.2.2 Some Other Important Considerations

2.2.2.1 Trade-Offs

A strategic choice inherently involves trade-offs. An organization is rarely able to be everything to everyone, and different customers or constituents may be willing to pay for or at least support different attributes of the same product or value proposition.

It is easy to observe this phenomenon in air travel. While some customers may feel underserved by current airline offerings, other customers may feel overserved and wish to pay a lower price for less services. Such distinct segmentation allows for discount airlines, such as Southwest Airlines or Ryanair, to compete for these latter customers. By accepting trade-offs, these airlines are able to offer stripped down air travel without the usual frills of meals or first-class seating.

Trade-offs are also necessary because different segments of the market may require the attention of different types of products, skills, organizational structures, or a combination thereof. For example, financial advisory firm Edward Jones prides itself on serving fiscally conservative customers, who typically prefer to consult with their personal advisors face-to-face. Because Edward Jones maintains a focus on this specific customer segment, the firm must thereby make trade-offs in its talent and organizational structure. As a key decision, Edward Jones chooses to recruit entrepreneurial-minded financial advisors who must each manage their own branch office. These advisors then have the independence and flexibility to spend quality time with customers within the confines of a pleasant office environment.

Companies that constantly come up with radically changing strategies that stray from their core value proposition often end up with too broad of a product or service. As a consequence, these companies are easily surpassed by rivals who have wisely adapted themselves to specific segments or conditions of the market. Thus, companies with strong competitive advantages accept uniqueness and openly celebrate trade-offs as they mold their best practices. As Southwest Airlines and Ryanair visibly demonstrate, what your organization chooses not to do can be even more essential to its distinctive value proposition than what your organization chooses to do. While your organization may hesitate to forego being the top ranked in all attributes, this sacrifice may actually help your organization excel at the attributes that you do target.

An added benefit of trade-offs is that they substantially deter imitation. Each trade-off your organization makes incrementally raises the cost of replication. Subsequently, as the number of trade-offs increases and the costs associated with imitation significantly amplify, competitors will begrudgingly realize that they cannot easily mimic your strategy.

As you choose between different strategic options, remember to take note of the following fundamental trade-offs and identify which will be your "secret ingredients:" product or service, countries, location, and team organization.

- Product or service: Will you be offering one type or many types? Will you respond to local needs through customization, or will you commit to efficiency through global standardization?
- Countries: Should you offer your product or service in just one country for the sake of simplicity, or will you offer it to numerous countries for variety? Will the countries where you offer your product or service allow you to maintain comparable operating environments, or will these operating environments contrast? Telecommunications company Nokia recently faced this latter question. Constrained by finite resources and energy, management decided to maintain comparable operating environments between countries and thereby faced the choice to move their business towards emerging markets or else focus on their existing market share in developed countries. After carrying out a thorough analysis of the market, Nokia believed that the emerg-

ing markets were well worth pursuing; therefore, management chose to shift their attention towards this realm.

■ Location: Where should you locate your headquarters or R&D centers? To minimize the effort spent on oversight, should you have one central location or many? Would you move your offices from one place to the next based on dynamic arbitrage, or would you maintain a static position?

■ Team organization: How should you structure your organization? Should you aim for standardization and coordination and thereby encourage management to exercise control, or should you introduce movement and the potential for chaos within your team structure by promoting decentralization and supporting the delegation of management control? Manufacturer Procter & Gamble struggled with organizational issues for many years, unable to settle on one structure for very long. Though parts of Procter & Gamble's organizational structure would, at times, encourage standardization and coordination, at other times the structure would promote decentralization causing confusion and widespread disruption throughout the company ranks.

2.2.2.2 Strategic Fit

As you deliberate among these trade-offs, it is key to choose the strategy that best fits your organization. Keep in mind that no strategy within an industry is *the* best strategy. Instead, in order to move your organization forward, it is essential that you assess your own (or in this world economy, outsourced) resources and strengths over which you can maintain well-guarded control.

Additionally, your strategic choices should fit with one another. The most common way to accomplish this is to develop two or three distinct sets of integrated strategic options. As you research the array of plausible options, flesh out the implications of each. The set of choices with the most positive implications will likely be the best one to choose. The ice cream company Ben & Jerry's employed this technique as they shaped various sets of options around offering a great-tasting ice cream versus a "hippy," all-natural ice cream. Ultimately, they chose the option that combined their delicious-tasting ice cream with a social mission dedicated to Earth-friendly innovations and sustainable living. This unique value proposition and marketing angle helped Ben & Jerry's amass millions in sales annually, leading to a successful acquisition by Unilever, where it continues to thrive. Thus, the foresight Ben & Jerry's demonstrated as it investigated its strategic options facilitated the success it benefits from today.

2.3 From Core Competency to Value Creation

2.3.1 Core Competency and Value Chain

Earlier, we explored the key components of a business strategy and advocated having a distinctive value proposition that clearly defines (1) what needs you will meet,

(2) which customers or constituents you will serve, and (3) what relative price, if applicable, you will charge. However, this alone is not enough to yield a sustainable competitive advantage.

2.3.1.1 Core Competency

The next thing we recommend that you identify in your organization is its core competency. In other words, what strength does your organization particularly possess? Whether it is in the form of processes, technical know-how, or strong relationships with suppliers, your core competency ultimately forms the basis of how your organization can add value.

Originally developed by C. K. Prahalad and Gary Hamel, the concept of a core competency,[1] or what an organization knows how to do the best, generally fulfills the following criteria:

1. It can be repeatedly leveraged for different markets and products.
2. It must contribute to the benefits experienced by end users.
3. It is difficult for peers to replicate.

Note that in order for it to be considered a core competence, customers also must value this strength. Specific examples of core competencies include:

- UPS's and FedEx's superb management of supply chain logistics.
- Sony's ability to manufacture consumer products that merge innovative designs with microelectronics.
- BMW's comprehension of efficient dynamics, through the product development of transmissions, engines, and other power train components.
- Expedia's exceptional understanding of technology within the online travel space.

By determining and sometimes adapting or modifying your organization's core competency and comprehending how best to enable and valorize it, you will know what will facilitate your business strategy and, in turn, your organization's business activities and processes.

Knowing your organization's core competency also will allow you to determine if your organization's attempt at diversification will succeed, depending on whether or not the changes continue to be closely linked to the organization's core competency, resulting in either an adjoint or disjoint diversification strategy (Figure 2.2).

Along this line, Mark Zuckerberg, CEO of Facebook, was quoted in the *Wall Street Journal* on September 12, 2012, dismissing the idea that Facebook should offer its own smartphones. Knowing that Facebook's core competency, which he wishes to maintain, resides in the system that the company has built to connect people around the world, Zuckerberg explicitly indicated that building a mobile phone to compete with Apple or Google would be a very wrong strategy for Facebook.[2]

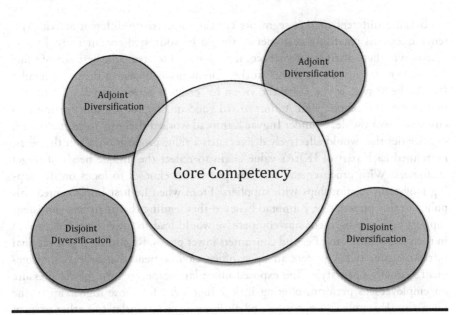

Figure 2.2   Core competency and diversification strategies.

2.3.1.2 *Value Chain*

Knowing your core competency will enable you to focus on such and such activities or processes, relationships, and knowledge, also known as your organization's value chain, to make it unique. Originally developed by Harvard Business School professor Michael Porter, this value chain consists of a sequence of primary activities and support activities that ultimately connect to best deliver your organization's core value proposition.[3]

According to Porter, an organization's primary activities consist of inbound logistics, operations, outbound logistics, sales and marketing, and after-sales services. As the organization's product passes through each of these primary activities, the product gains added value. Meanwhile, Porter maintains, the support activities that help an organization reinforce these primary activities consist of firm infrastructure, human resources management, technology development, and procurement. By ensuring that these primary and support activities leverage your core competency, you can ultimately differentiate your organization from its rivals.

Altogether, this chain of activities should provide more value to the organization's product than the sum of the value added by each individual activity. Because each part of the value chain affects another, it is essential to carefully think through the resulting interactions. For example, how will human resources cooperate within the organization's infrastructure? Will technology development enable procurement? Do operations facilitate inbound and outbound logistics? Should marketing and sales lend to after-sales service?

Because different market segments typically necessitate different activity systems, questions regarding customer fit should be addressed concurrently. In particular, will these distinct activities combine together to create the best mix of value for your chosen market segment? In the aforementioned case of furniture retailer IKEA, the answer is yes. With the vision to "create a better everyday life for the majority of the people," IKEA aims to sell good-quality yet low-cost furniture to customers worldwide. Founder Ingvar Kamprad worked tirelessly to craft a system of activities that would effectively deliver such a value proposition. Over the years, he refined each part of IKEA's value chain to reflect the unique needs of target customers. With procurement, for example, IKEA chooses to focus on developing long-term relationships with suppliers. From when he first implemented this policy to this present day, Kamprad believed that lending their partners consistent support and helping them stay competitive would lead to lower costs that would in turn allow IKEA to offer end consumers lower prices. Regarding organizational infrastructure, IKEA prefers an open office environment that reflects management's equally open style. The exposed office landscape, in turn, places pressure on employees to perform, offering little refuge even for those higher up in the hierarchy. This policy of openness and antibureaucracy translates to other parts of IKEA's value chain, and facilitates a nimble organizational structure that can more effectively execute its vision.[4]

2.3.2 Relative Cost Analysis

In addition to identifying your organization's value chain, performing a relative cost analysis can help you to further refine your organization's competitive advantage. By directly comparing your organization's unit costs, where applicable, with those of your competitors, you may gain a better understanding of your business model and determine where you can lower costs.

Carrying out such an analysis can bolster your viewpoint on a number of strategic and tactical issues. Using Figure 2.3 as an example, you can easily determine in what areas competitors have a greater cost advantage and, therefore, what drives their profitability. As you conduct a side-by-side comparison with your own unit costs, you can decide where to focus your cost reduction efforts.

For example, analyzing Figure 2.3 reveals that Competitor B's material costs are $0.15 less per unit than those of your organization. Taking note of this difference, it may be worthwhile to reexamine your raw material inputs and determine whether you can lower the associated costs without affecting the quality of your final product. You could potentially decrease raw material usage, streamline inventory management, or renovate your purchasing process. Implementing such improvements could amount to millions of dollars saved annually and a dramatic boost to your business's profitability, or if your organization is a nonprofit, provide a significant competitive advantage against other nonprofits.

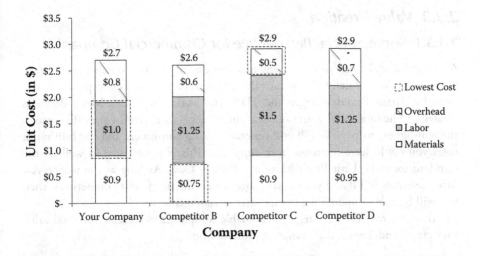

Figure 2.3   Relative cost analysis.

You can employ a detailed, bottom-up approach to perform the relative cost analysis found in Figure 2.3. As you conduct primary and secondary research, you can derive or triangulate the major cost drivers of your competitors. To facilitate this process, begin by mapping out the value chain in which you and your competitors engage, charting the process by which the raw materials become the final product, from end-to-end.

Next, identify the costs tied to each activity within the value chain. You may need to access multiple sources in order to arrive at each approximate figure. To comprehend your competitor's raw material or packaging costs, for example, you may need to research industry reports or speak with knowledgeable purchasing managers and suppliers. To understand what drives direct labor or overhead costs, you may want to research job postings, speak with operations managers, or conduct plant tours where you can further note staffing, machine utilization, speeds, and maintenance. Finally, to uncover administrative, sales, and marketing cost drivers, you may need to retrieve 10-K filings, contact human resources, meet with sales managers, and speak with investor relations or marketing team members. As you comb these sources for cost data, it is important to maintain a creative mindset yet behave ethically.

As earlier noted, when you build up costs activity by activity, you will be able to calculate where your organization might have cost disadvantages relative to your competitors. You thereafter can determine what activities have the most significant potential for cost savings and focus your reduction efforts on these areas accordingly. Once you improve your cost position, you may be able to take advantage of the resulting benefits, such as by allocating the amount you captured in cost savings toward enhancing your brand image or investing in innovation efforts.

2.3.3 Value Creation

2.3.3.1 Some Special Perspective for Commercial Companies

As a commercial company, your organization can maintain a competitive advantage by consistently delivering great value to your customers. A concept first developed by Adam Brandenburger and Harborne Stuart in "Value-Based Business Strategy,"[5] the total value your organization creates is measured by the difference in the willingness-to-pay (WTP) you generate among consumers and the minimum costs you could have incurred from suppliers. This is represented as well by the standard formula: Unit Profit Margin = Price − Cost. As long as the wedge you drive between WTP and your costs is greater than that of your competitors, then you will be able to maintain a competitive advantage.

There are four basic strategies that enable companies to increase the total value they create and, hence, their range of profitability:

1. Product or service differentiation
2. Low cost
3. Customer relationship
4. Network effect

If your organization chooses to follow a differentiation strategy, then you can drive up WTP among your customers by leveraging the unique qualities of your product or service to raise prices. Be cautious, however, as you can likely expect to incur commensurate costs. Thus, as you make progress on the top part of the wedge, it is important to account for the bottom part as well and ensure that the costs you are adding to your activities directly contribute to your WTP.

On the other hand, if your organization pursues a low cost strategy, then you must optimize your costs by finding the minimum price that your suppliers are willing to accept. However, as the saying goes, you get what you pay for. If lower costs translate into lower quality supplies for your final product, then you may be sacrificing commensurate WTP. Thus, as you make progress on the bottom part of the wedge, you must ensure that your final product still meets the minimum requirements expected by consumers. Ways in which you can achieve such low costs, without necessarily sacrificing quality, include continuously improving your organization's operating efficiency, leveraging your superior supply chain, or innovatively redesigning your product or service.

As another option, your organization may prefer to follow a customer relationship strategy. The success of this strategy relies on the strength of the personal relationships your organization is able to build with its customer base. These customers appreciate the value they receive from their long-standing relationships with your employees, with benefits ranging from personalized services to customized solutions. These customers' resulting loyalty to your business drives up WTP.

Lastly, your organization may pursue a network effect strategy, otherwise known as a winner-take-all strategy. A relatively new phenomenon, the network effect occurs when more and more of a product is sold, thereby increasing the resulting network of users, which in turn increases the value of the product. In other words, with network effects, there are greater benefits for the user as the total number of the product's users rises. Online auction site eBay is an example of an organization that successfully leveraged the network effect strategy. Though other auction sites had existed long before, eBay was able to attract its first buyers and sellers by enabling them to easily purchase or sell products on the site. As eBay continued to gain popularity, more buyers began frequenting the site because sellers were already listing the products they desired. Concurrently, more sellers began to use the site because so many buyers were already arriving in search of their next purchase. Consequently, eBay rapidly grew to become the dominant player in its industry and continued to maintain this position until the rise of Amazon.

Whichever strategy you pursue, you must continue to improve your position at both ends of the wedge in order to further enhance your competitive advantage.

2.3.3.2 Some Special Perspective for Nonprofit Organizations

While WTP may be relevant for commercial companies, you should and would not use WTP for nonprofit organizations. For these, a set of criteria different than the cost should be identified to determine what constitutes value for the nonprofit organization's donors or volunteers or, more broadly speaking, constituents.

Examples of such criteria could be, in some cases, the number of patients who are saved from a specific cancer type or still the percentage of students who successfully get into college from the state of New York.

2.4 Michael Porter's Five Forces Framework

When it comes to business strategy formulation, there may be no other author who is more known than Professor Michael Porter with his Five Forces framework.

2.4.1 Michael Porter's Five Forces

Steering your organization toward strong positions within your industry or social sector and away from weak ones is crucial to your profitability or success. Thus, we will spend this next section helping you understand the underlying economics of an industry or area of competition. Gaining such knowledge should enable you to distinguish whether your industry is structurally attractive with high, long-term profit potential or unattractive with low, short-term profit potential—and then decide where and how to best compete.

Originally developed by Porter, the Five Forces framework allows you to thoroughly examine an industry from different dimensions. These Five Forces include:[6]

1. The bargaining power of suppliers
2. The bargaining power of customers
3. The threat of new entrants
4. The threat of substitutes
5. The rivalry among existing competitors

2.4.1.1 Bargaining Power of Suppliers

In any given industry, there may exist several suppliers, such as equipment providers and labor providers (human capital). The more power these suppliers are able to exert over an organization, the less attractive the industry is.

In what ways can suppliers exert power? That depends on how easily they are able to raise prices, shift costs downstream, and limit the quality of goods and services they provide. Each of these factors can dramatically erode the profitability of an industry and, thus, render it unattractive.

2.4.1.2 Bargaining Power of Customers

As with suppliers, the more powerful the customers are, the less attractive an industry is. These customers can especially demonstrate power when they are price sensitive or have clout.

Why does a customer exhibit price sensitivity? When a company within an industry is business-to-business (B2B) and their customer base consists of other companies, this customer base can be especially price sensitive when the quality of their own products remains unaffected by the industry's product. In addition, customers frequently find that certain purchases represent a significant fraction of their costs. Thus, if a customer group maintains generally low profits, an increase in a product's price may cause customers to alter their purchase habits and seek a lower cost substitute.

To increase their bargaining power, customers can command clout by offering standardized products. Standardization of products requires standardization of input materials, meaning that customers can more easily carry out concentrated, high-volume purchasing. Customers also can command clout by exhibiting a credible threat to integrate backwards: If an organization fears that the customer has the ability to bring the organization's product in-house, then the customer is able to wield additional power. Customers also can command greater clout if there are few switching costs associated with the industry and a customer can easily go from one organization's product to another without having to overcome too many obstacles, such as added charges or inconvenience.

2.4.1.3 Threat of New Entrants

The threat of new entrants is largely dependent on an industry's barriers to entry. The higher the barriers to entry, the more difficult it is for new companies to enter an industry.

One common barrier to entry is capital requirements. If it takes a lot of initial capital for a new entrant to launch, especially due to the high cost of equipment or customer acquisition, then movement into the industry will be hindered. Conversely, industries with low barriers encourage entry. You may be surprised to learn, for example, that it does not take much capital to begin your own airline; and because of this low barrier to entry, the airline industry regularly suffers from new entrants and an ever-evolving competitive landscape.

Another barrier to entry involves switching costs for customers, as previously mentioned. If switching from one organization's products to another is so simple that customers can readily do so without much financial or logistical complication, then this will facilitate new entrants' success within the industry.

Other key barriers to entry include: incumbency advantages, such as proprietary technology and existing relationships; government policy that may impose restrictive regulatory obstacles; and unequal access to distribution channels.

2.4.1.4 Threat of Substitutes

Substitutes are products that can perform either the same or a similar function as another product, albeit different means. A publishing house's books, for example, can be substituted by other reading formats, such as magazines and newspapers, or by other means of entertainment, such as movies, music, television, or surfing the Internet. Consumers are able to use any of these products to fill their leisure hours, making the competition among book publishers high. Thus, the greater the number of potential substitutes identified within an industry, the less attractive the industry is.

2.4.1.5 Rivalry among Existing Competitors

An industry generally becomes less attractive as the intensity of the rivalry among existing competitors increases. Thus, it is imperative to remain aware of the factors that can drive this competition. Evidently, a high number of competitors will promote antagonism within an industry, but sluggish industry growth and high exit barriers also can enhance rivalry as companies find themselves forced to remain within an industry and compete for a shrinking piece of the pie.

Existing rivalry can have a deep impact on an industry's overall profit potential, largely depending on the basis on which companies compete. Price wars, in particular, will frequently drive the overall profit of an industry downwards. When companies compete on price, it is typically because the product lacks differentiation or is perishable. Otherwise, the temptation to compete on price also may be driven by high fixed costs and low marginal costs, or by an inability to expand capacity except in large increments, consequently encouraging the pursuit of high sales volume at the risk of cutting prices.

For illustrative purposes, let us examine the Five Forces with respect to Walmart, the American multinational retailer, and the Museum of Modern Art (MoMA), the nonprofit art museum in New York City.

2.4.1.6 Walmart and Porter's Five Forces

2.4.1.6.1 Bargaining Power of Suppliers

Walmart represents a large portion of their suppliers' overall sales. As a result, suppliers possess a very limited ability to set prices and Walmart is able to bargain down its costs.

2.4.1.6.2 Bargaining Power of Customers

Walmart's customers possess limited power. Walmart generally participates in the standardization of its products, offering products that are similar nationwide and have limited local focus. Walmart can thus purchase select product lines from suppliers at high volumes and low costs, which in turn allows it to set low prices in comparison to the rest of the industry. Walmart also is frequently one of the few players within the smaller markets. Therefore, customers located in these markets may experience deep inconvenience if they attempt to shop at a retailer located farther away.

2.4.1.6.3 Threat of New Entrants

Walmart's large-scale business model severely limits the opportunity for other companies to enter. Those who do enter risk instant price retaliation by Walmart and hence potential bankruptcy. Walmart also benefits from the barriers formed by the high fixed costs required to develop stores and the long timeframe it takes to establish solid relationships with suppliers.

2.4.1.6.4 Threat of Substitutes

Online retailers, such as Amazon, could easily pose a threat to Walmart in several product categories due to online retailers' relative convenience and reliability.

However, given Walmart's economies of scale, smaller brick-and-mortar stores would be unlikely to serve as viable substitutes.

2.4.1.6.5 Rivalry among Existing Competitors

Walmart faces somewhat strong rivalry from other industry players like Kmart, which sells products across similar segments. However, these companies largely compete on price, thereby positioning Walmart at a competitive advantage since Walmart can leverage its superior supply chain management and large-scale business model to offer the lowest prices. One rival retailer that does not compete on price and thereby succeeds in co-existing with Walmart is Target. Indeed, Target differentiates itself by competing on the basis of their higher-quality brand and more attractive customer experience.

As exemplified by the Five Forces, from Walmart's perspective, the industry is altogether structurally attractive.

2.4.1.7 The MoMA and Porter's Five Forces

2.4.1.7.1 Bargaining Power of Suppliers

In the case of the MoMA, the influential museum has collected thousands of artworks among its libraries and archives, including sculptures, paintings, drawings, and photographs. With such an expansive collection of modern masterpieces, including Vincent van Gogh's *The Starry Night* and Andy Warhol's *Campbell's Soup Cans*, as well as the museum's associated prestige, few suppliers of art can wield significant negotiating power over the MoMA. As a result, the MoMA holds much leverage during its arts acquisition process.

2.4.1.7.2 Bargaining Power of Customers

The MoMA's customers (in this instance, museum visitors) also possess limited bargaining power. Though the MoMA aims to be accessible to the entire public, the organization may nonetheless charge an admission fee of its choosing without much repercussion. Its unparalleled collection of rare artwork offers the MoMA strong leverage over what it can charge its visitors. Reflecting this reality, the MoMA has steadily increased its admission prices over the past decade; and in September 2011, it became the second arts institution in the United States to charge $25 for adults.[7] Despite occasional negative press for these fee hikes, the public has ultimately adjusted, as evidenced by the subsequent record growth in visitors.

The MoMA also earns revenue from membership dues, retail operations, and publishing operations as other sources of support. Due to the MoMA's significant brand equity, the museum wields significant leverage in these verticals, leaving customers little bargaining power.

2.4.1.7.3 Threat of New Entrants

The MoMA does not have to fear new entrants. A large amount of capital is required to acquire quality works of art and build an exhibition space. In addition, a considerable amount of reputation-building is necessary to foster credibility among the art community and potential visitors alike. As a result, new entrants would find it difficult to enter the industry at a scale large enough to compete with the MoMA.

2.4.1.7.4 Threat of Substitutes

All other forms of entertainment or art-related exhibitions may serve as potential substitutes for the MoMA, ranging from new art galleries to Broadway shows and films at the movie theater. Thus, the MoMA must continue to provide distinctive offerings, such as special exhibits or limited engagements, which can repeatedly draw visitors away from these potential substitutes.

2.4.1.7.5 Rivalry among Existing Competitors

Although the MoMA faces strong rivalry from existing museums that are based in New York City, the MoMA still remains at the top of its class. While the Metropolitan Museum of Art, the Guggenheim Museum, and the Whitney Museum present comparable offerings, the specific pieces of art within the MoMA's collection allow for the museum to offer unique value to visitors that cannot be easily replaced.

In all, according to the Five Forces, the industry is structurally attractive from the MoMA's perspective.

2.4.2 Leading Uses of the Five Forces Framework

Regardless of whether you are a for-profit or nonprofit executive, your role is to steer your organization toward a superior position within your given industry or social sector. While using the Five Forces framework will help you to distinguish between structurally attractive and unattractive industries, the ultimate benefit of understanding the Five Forces is that your organization may use this knowledge to stake out a position that is less vulnerable to these forces and build up defenses accordingly.

In other words, leveraging the framework will increase your organization's ability to exploit industry change as dynamic shifts occur among new entrants, substitutes, suppliers, customers, and existing rivals. You will be able to recognize and prioritize the impact of these external changes on your organization's strategy as well as the industry or social sector's attractiveness. Being able to perceive and capture these new, promising positions will ideally result in a first-mover advantage.

Within the newspaper industry, the *Wall Street Journal* comprehended the future impact of technology on the demands of its customers and, as a result, expanded its capabilities online in advance of its competition, using the Internet as a tool to increase circulation and audience engagement. The majority of competitors who initially failed to take similar actions eventually followed suit, but nonetheless still lag far behind the *Wall Street Journal* in terms of online capabilities and readership presently. Taking such steps allowed for the *Wall Street Journal* to influence the Five Forces and guide the industry toward new ways of competing, thereby reshaping the industry structure.

2.4.3 A Sixth Force

Though Michael Porter's Five Forces remains one of the most known strategic frameworks, other authors have since identified ways to improve upon it. Among them are academics Gerry Johnson, Kevan Scholes, and Richard Whittington.

According to Johnson, Scholes, and Whittington, there is a sixth force that is not commonly acknowledged, but which highlights the power of complements.[8] A complement is a product that is used in conjunction with an industry's product, such as a razor and blades, or a racquet and tennis balls. From an organization's perspective, the availability of complements can augment the demand for its product. As a result, complements, by and large, enhance the attractiveness of an industry.

2.5 Product–Market Growth Directions Matrix

While we believe that utilizing Porter's Five Forces is a solid step on the path to strategy development, planning for concrete long-term growth may require additional analysis. One such analysis can be performed using Figure 2.4, which is a revision of the Product–Market Growth Matrix originally created by Igor Ansoff.[9]

What is shown in Figure 2.4 is an organization's present position in the market and its potential opportunities for growth and diversification, based on various combinations of markets and products or services. If your organization would like to expand, it must take advantage of its current position by assessing its existing

		Current	Modified	New
Market	Current	Market penetration	Partial product/service diversification	Product development
	New	Market development	Partial market diversification	Diversification
		Current	Modified	New
			Product/Service	

Figure 2.4   Product–Market Growth Directions Matrix.

resources and capacity for growth. From there, it has the opportunity to expand in different directions: (1) market penetration, (2) market development, (3) partial product/service diversification, (4) partial market diversification, (5) product development, and (6) full diversification.

If your organization remains in its present position, selling its current product or service within its current market, then your organization may continue to grow through market penetration, improving the product (through cost-cutting, for example) or encouraging customers to further increase their usage (by deriving new ways in which the product can be used, for example). In this scenario, revenue growth based on the sales of your current product or service will become critical to your organization's continued success. Likewise, profit margins also must improve for your organization to thrive. You will have to exercise better control over your costs than competitors and consistently manage how much of every dollar in revenue your organization actually retains in earnings.

Alternatively, your organization could pursue a new direction through market development, selling its current product or service within a new market. This strategy might be achieved by targeting a different customer segment or by expanding your geographical focus. This type of expansion could involve significant effort from your marketing team as they target new customers through advertising campaigns on traditional or online channels.

On the other hand, your organization could pursue partial product/service diversification by somewhat modifying its current offering and selling this modified product/service to its current market or a subset of the market. Otherwise, if your organization chooses to sell this modified product to a completely new market, then this is referred to as partial market diversification. Though not pictured in Figure 2.4, there is a hybrid possibility as well. Your organization also could sell this modified product to both its current and new markets, which would move your organization squarely in the middle of the cells labeled "partial product/service diversification" and "partial market diversification" in Figure 2.4.

As another option, your organization could remain in its current market, but innovate to introduce a new product through product development. Developing an offering with new options or features could renew attention from your loyal customer base and move your organization onto an upward growth trajectory.

As a final option, your organization may aim to move into new, potentially unfamiliar markets with an entirely new product through full diversification. This strategy for growth requires a longer-term mindset, yet you should maintain a clear sense of what is actually feasible, based on your present position.

Regardless of which direction your organization moves, the rate of growth achieved will not only depend on the organization's resources and capacity for expansion, but also on the average rate of change within the organization's given industry. To be realistic about this growth, it is important to next understand the tailored activities and financial numbers that drive such goals.

2.6 The Strategy Blade

The Strategy Blade is an additional tool for business strategy and value creation, which can vary across organizations. Different organizations may place different activities within their respective Strategy Blades, based on importance. To this effect, because the activities that make up a Strategy Blade must fit the organization's culture and values, an organization must determine the nuances that drive its strategy. Likewise, if an organization places particular emphasis on one activity over another, then the size of that activity as shown on the Blade should reflect its importance. For example, while there may be an emphasis on professional services and IT for the firm in Figure 2.5, another organization may not place professional services on the Strategy Blade at all.

In short, the Strategy Blade should not be treated as a checklist. Instead, the Strategy Blade should be used to focus on what truly makes your business different by assessing where your organization currently is at while also visualizing where it could go. Thus, rather than turning this into an exercise wherein you list

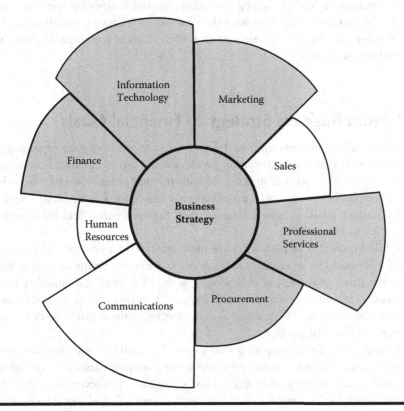

Figure 2.5　Strategy Blade.

the standard activities that are typically connected to a commercial or nonprofit organization's strategy, challenge yourself to really reflect on how each part of the Blade works with the others—and then elucidate what it would take to move your organization ahead of its competitors.

Imagine, for example, that after utilizing the Product-Market Growth Directions Matrix, you decide to focus on an additional customer segment: After reviewing your Strategy Blade, would you want to do anything differently? If you shifted towards this different market, consider if any of the activities within your Strategy Blade could ultimately do more for your organization. Perhaps this move to acquire additional customers would allow for your procurement team to gain additional bargaining power when purchasing from suppliers, lowering the cost of goods sold on a per unit basis. Or perhaps there are specific marketing plans that, when altered to include these additional target customers, could better promote your product or service overall. In the end, the basic idea is to have a cohesive set of plans that helps propagate your organization ahead of the competition and drives its business strategy forward.

By continuously elaborating on these thoughts and sharpening your responses, you should ultimately be able to not only comprehend what your organization does well and does not do well, but also envision what facets of your organization set— or *could* set—it apart.

2.7 From Business Strategy to Financial Goals

Regardless of how an organization defines its future business goals or strategy, it is fundamental that the organization provides some specific financial projections for what it wants to achieve in terms of both revenue generation and cost reduction. Examples of such financial projections are shown for a commercial company via its business goals, income statement, cash flow statement, and balance sheet (Figure 2.6 to Figure 2.9).

While Figure 2.6 to Figure 2.9 are more relevant to a commercial company, Figure 2.10 would be an example that is more relevant to a nonprofit association.

As discussed in the rest of this book, it is the IT leaders' responsibility to use the financial statements such as those in Figure 2.6 to Figure 2.10 as a guideline to see how effectively the IT roadmap is contributing to the organization's business strategy and financial goals.

This said, we are not implying that a good IT roadmap or department alone will necessarily enable a commercial company or a nonprofit association to achieve all of its business strategy and financial goals. Instead, as believers in modern and creative technology, we mean to say that a well-aligned IT roadmap should be able to make a significant contribution to an organization's business strategy or social objectives—along with the support of other departments' roadmaps.

Business Goals Projections

Items	Base Year	Year 1	Year 2	Year 3
Annual revenue growth rate	20%	20%	20%	20%
Revenue	$1,750,000	$2,100,000	$2,520,000	$3,024,000
Cost of goods sold (as % of revenue)	50%	50%	45%	40%
Cost of goods sold	–$875,000	–$1,050,000	–$1,134,000	–$1,209,600
Sales & marketing expenses (as % of revenue)	14%	14%	14%	14%
General & administrative expenses (as % of revenue)	6%	6%	6%	6%
Depreciation expenses	–$10,000	–$10,000	–$10,000	–$20,000
Tax rate	35%	35%	35%	35%

Figure 2.6   Example of business goals.

On a related note, while it is strongly recommended that you use this discussion on business strategy to develop roadmaps for marketing, supply chain, and other key organization departments, for the purposes of this book, we will be only focusing on the IT roadmap throughout the remainder of this book.

2.8 Takeaways

As you develop your business strategy, ensure that it satisfies the following criteria: internal consistency, external consistency, and dynamic consistency. At the same time, forge a value proposition that resolves what needs and which customers or constituents your organization will serve and at what price. Understand that you may have to make trade-offs as you decide on your product or service, which countries you will provide this offering, your location of operations, and your team's organization. Nonetheless, always ensure that these strategic choices fit with one another.

Next, it is important to identify the organization's core competency, defined as what the organization does best to meet its given strategy. This will enable to you to

Pro Forma Income Statement

	Base Year	Year 1	Year 2	Year 3
Revenue	**$1,750,000**	**$2,100,000**	**$2,520,000**	**$3,024,000**
Raw materials	−105,000	−126,000	−151,200	−181,440
Direct labor costs	−770,000	−924,000	−982,800	−1,028,160
Cost of goods sold	**−$875,000**	**−$1,050,000**	**−$1,134,000**	**−$1,209,600**
Gross profit	**$875,000**	**$1,050,000**	**$1,386,000**	**$1,814,400**
Sales & marketing expenses	−245,000	−294,000	−352,800	−423,360
General & administrative expenses	−105,000	−126,000	−151,200	−181,440
Earnings before interest, taxes, depreciation & amortization	**$525,000**	**$630,000**	**$882,000**	**$1,209,600**
Depreciation expenses	−10,000	−10,000	−10,000	−20,000
Operating profit	**$515,000**	**$620,000**	**$872,000**	**$1,189,600**
Interest expense (net)	−34,000	−24,650	−10,625	−3,613
Pretax income	**$481,000**	**$595,350**	**$861,375**	**$1,185,988**
Income taxes	−168,350	−208,373	−301,481	−415,096
Net income	**$312,650**	**$386,978**	**$559,894**	**$770,892**

Figure 2.7 Pro forma income statement.

develop your organization's value chain, or the set of activities that will ultimately connect to best deliver your organization's core value proposition.

To further refine your organization's competitive advantage, you should next analyze your organization's unit costs and compare them with those of your competitors in order to determine where to focus your cost reduction efforts. Ultimately, to maintain a competitive advantage, the difference between your organization's

Pro Forma Cash Flow Statement

		Base Year	Year 1	Year 2	Year 3
Net income			**$386,978**	**$559,894**	**$770,892**
Depreciation			10,000	10,000	20,000
Changes in working capital					
	Account receivable		86,301	−69,041	−82,849
	Inventory		−32,219	−17,951	−17,398
	Accounts payable		15,822	13,808	15,534
Cash from operating activities			**$466,882**	**$496,710**	**$706,178**
Capital expenditures			−10,000	−10,000	−20,000
Other investment			0	0	0
Cash from investing activities			**−$10,000**	**−$10,000**	**−$20,000**
Net borrowing			−275,000	−137,500	−68,750
Dividends			0	0	0
Capital contributions			0	0	0
Cash from financing activities			**−$275,000**	**−$137,500**	**−$68,750**
Change in cash			**$181,882**	**$349,210**	**$617,428**

Figure 2.8 Pro forma cash flow statement.

Pro Forma Balance Sheet

	Base Year	Year 1	Year 2	Year 3
Assets				
Cash and cash equivalents	$876,825	$1,058,706	$1,407,917	$2,025,345
Accounts receivable	431,507	345,205	414,247	497,096
Inventories	161,096	193,315	211,266	228,664
Total current assets	**$1,469,428**	**$1,597,227**	**$2,033,429**	**$2,751,105**
Property, plant, and equipment	100,000	100,000	100,000	100,000
Goodwill	72,332	72,332	72,332	72,332
Total assets	**$1,641,760**	**$1,769,559**	**$2,205,761**	**$2,923,437**
Liabilities				
Accounts payable	$79,110	$94,932	$108,740	$124,274
Debt	500,000	225,000	87,500	18,750
Total liabilities	**$579,110**	**$319,932**	**$196,240**	**$143,024**
Stockholders' equity				
Starting stockholders' equity	$750,000	$1,062,650	$1,449,628	$2,009,521
Net income	312,650	386,978	559,894	770,892
Dividends	0	0	0	0
Capital contributions	0	0	0	0
Stockholders' equity	**$1,062,650**	**$1,449,628**	**$2,009,521**	**$2,780,413**
Total liabilities & equity	**$1,641,760**	**$1,769,559**	**$2,205,761**	**$2,923,437**

Figure 2.9   Pro forma balance sheet.

costs and the willingness-to-pay it generates among customers should be greater than that of your competitors. There are four basic strategies that your organization could pursue to increase the total value it creates and, hence, its range of profitability: product or service differentiation, low cost, customer relationship, or network effect.

Revenues	Base Year	Year 1	Year 2	Year 3
Special events	$20,000	$30,000	$40,000	$50,000
Sponsorships of illiterate children	52,000	54,600	58,968	64,865
Sales of books written by children	154,000	161,700	177,870	204,550
Fundraising campaign from institutional donors	244,000	256,200	269,010	282,460
Fundraising campaign from individual donors	45,000	50,000	50,000	50,000
Government grant	25,000	25,000	25,000	25,000
Total revenue	**$540,000**	**$577,500**	**$620,848**	**$676,875**

Figure 2.10   Example of revenue projections.

In addition, utilize the Five Forces framework, Product–Market Growth Directions Matrix, and the strategy wheel to identify where and how to best compete within your given industry or social sector, in order to set your organization apart.

Last but not least, your organization should provide specific financial projections for what it would like to achieve in terms of both revenue generation and cost reduction. It is then the IT leaders' responsibility to use these financial statements as a guideline to see how effectively the IT roadmap is contributing to the organization's business strategy and financial goals.

References

1. Hamel, G., and C. K. Prahalad. 1996. *Competing for the future.* Boston: Harvard Business Review Press.
2. Fowler, G. 2012. Zuckerberg admits to missteps. *Wall Street Journal,* September 12.
3. Porter, M. 1985. *Competitive advantage: Creating and sustaining superior performance.* New York: The Free Press.
4. Dahlvig, A. 2012. *The IKEA edge: Building global growth and social good at the world's most iconic home store.* New York: McGraw-Hill.
5. Brandenburger, A., and H. Stuart. 1996. Value-based business strategy. *The Massachusetts Institute of Technology Journal of Economics & Management Strategy* 5 (1): 10.
6. Porter, M. 1980. *Competitive strategy: Techniques for analyzing industries and competitors.* New York: The Free Press.
7. Souccar, M. K. 2011. MoMA raising admission fee. *Crain's New York,* July 28.
8. Johnson, G., K. Scholes, and R. Whittington. 2009. *Fundamentals of strategy.* London: FT Prentice Hall.
9. Ansoff, I. 1957. Strategies for diversification. *Harvard Business Review* 35 (5): 113–124.

AN INTRODUCTION TO LEAN, LEAN AND AGILE ORGANIZATION, AND LEAN AND AGILE IT

II

Because we are advocates of a Lean and Agile organization and a Lean and Agile IT to create more value and innovation for an organization, in the following pages, we are going to define what we mean by Lean (and, therefore, Agile), establishing the foundation for our discussion going forward.

Chapter 3

What Do We Mean by Lean, Lean and Agile Organization, and Lean and Agile IT?

3.1 Chapter Objective

This chapter introduces the reader to the concepts of Lean and, by way of consequence, Agile. We will then discuss the concept of a Lean and Agile organization, a Lean and Agile IT, and a Lean and Agile IT roadmap. To this effect, we will ultimately provide the reader with a summary of what it would mean for an organization, an IT department, and an IT roadmap to be Lean and Agile.

3.2 What Is Lean?

For the purpose of this book, we will consider Lean to be a catchphrase that describes a management approach originally invented by Taiichi Ohno and applied at Toyota in Japan after World War II. This catchphrase was eventually popularized by a team of MIT researchers working under the direction of James Womack, founder of Lean Enterprise Institute, Inc.

For Womack and Daniel Jones, there are five core principles of Lean, as described in their book *Lean Thinking,*[1] published in 1995. For them, these principles include:

1. **Value:** The main idea here is for providers to maximize customer value of a product or service, as defined by the customers.
2. **Value stream:** A value stream is a set of actions needed to bring a product to an organization's customers.
3. **Flow:** Flow is the seamless integration of value-added steps in a business process. Lean experts think they achieve flow when people and materials interact seamlessly and effortlessly. Making operations flow is the ultimate goal of Lean. When waste is reduced and the excess inventory is eliminated, you are left with work that effortlessly flows from start to finish.
4. **Pull:** A pull organization is one in which the supply chain sends a product through the supply chain because there is a specific demand for that one product pulled by the customers, as opposed to creating all the products first as inventory and "pushing" them out to distributors onto the customers.
5. **Perfection:** Perfection is achieved when the organization can create customer value, identify the value streams, make the work flow, and when customers pull the product from the providers' supply chain.

To follow Shigeo Shingo, who used to work with Ochii Ohno, the father of both the Toyota Production System (TPS) and Kanban, we can define seven types of waste:[2]

1. **Defects:** Any work product that fails to meet customer requirements is waste.
2. **Extra processing:** Any step within a process or team workflow that does not add any value is waste.
3. **Inventory:** Raw material, work-in-process, or a finished product that is not directly required to fulfill an order is waste.
4. **Motion:** Any movement by any team member that does not add any value to the process or team workflow is waste.
5. **Overproduction:** Producing more than is needed at any given time is waste.
6. **Transportation:** Any movement of products or materials between process or team workflow steps that is not needed is waste.
7. **Waiting:** When a worker within a process or workflow is waiting to carry out a task, his or her time is wasted.

In addition to these seven types of wastes, an eighth type of waste also was added and is known as the "underutilization of employees."

3.3 So What Do We Mean by a Lean and Agile Organization and a Lean and Agile IT and IT Roadmap?

By this, we mean any commercial or nonprofit organization that is both Lean and Agile and any IT department that operates as seamlessly and as effortlessly as possible at the lowest cost while bringing the maximum value to its customers or constituents.

More specifically, to be Lean and Agile, both the organization and its IT would need to:

- Focus more on value streams or enterprise business processes that create value for customers or constituents.
- Avoid duplication of processes, systems, and activities in general.
- Trust and believe in employees or team members.
- Leverage system thinking to see all connected parts, in order to better understand the consequence of a process or decision.
- Make process activities and steps and everything else visible.
- Increase customer value by reducing lead time while increasing the overall throughput and quality of the product or service to be delivered.
- Eliminate anything that does not bring value to the customer or constituent.
- Work by regular increments and avoid that teams have to multitask.
- Optimize to perfection (otherwise known as "Kaizen").

Unlike the traditional approach, where there was always an end state that people and companies had to strive to reach, Lean does not have an end state, but seeks, instead, to encourage continuous improvement (or perfection).

In addition to the above principles, a new Lean and Agile organization also should leverage IT as a primary activity, rather than a support activity.

This would mean, among other things, that the value chain should be modified to look like Figure 3.1, with IT cutting across all the primary activities. In other words, IT is itself a key activity as opposed to an afterthought.

Likewise, a new Lean and Agile organization should deliver products or services incrementally as a result of the close collaboration between everyone within the organization—especially between the business and IT when it comes to software development and delivery.

Ultimately, as you can see, Lean and Agile IT impacts not only IT, but also the business organization as a whole.

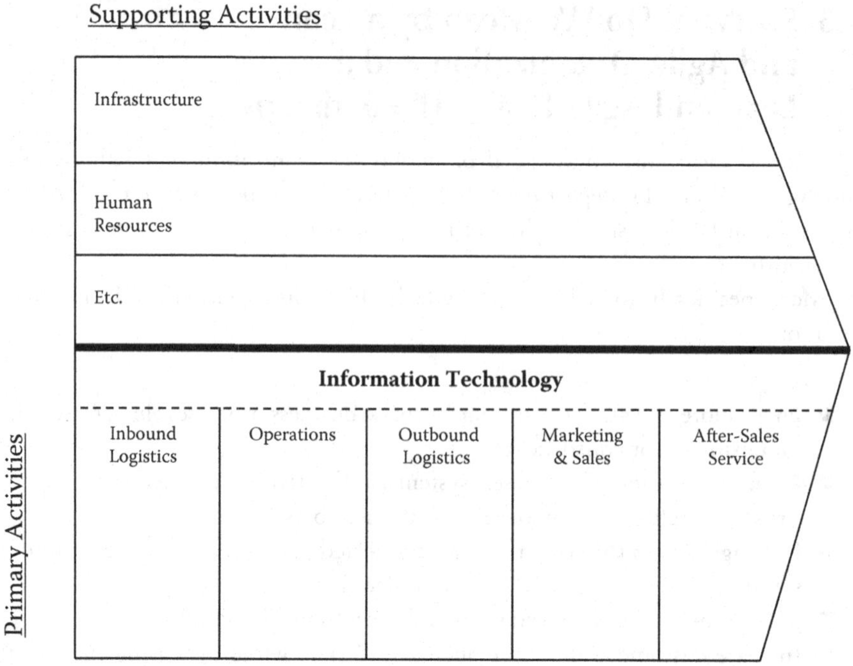

<u>Supporting Activities</u>

Figure 3.1 IT as a primary activity of the value chain.

3.4 Takeaways

This chapter helps you, the reader, better understand the concept of Lean and, therefore, Agile. This will subsequently help you recognize if your organization is a Lean and Agile organization and, likewise, if your organization's IT or IT roadmap is Lean and Agile.

For an organization to be Lean and Agile, it should:

■ Bring the most value to its customers or constituents.
■ Put emphasis on common enterprise processes over functional processes that are only needed by a department for its own activities.
■ Avoid creating overlapping or redundant activities, processes, and systems.
■ Continuously deliver value by delivering shippable products (which can be software systems) and services in increments.
■ Produce products (which can be software systems) or services of the highest level of quality.
■ Continuously adapt to the external changing environment.
■ Turn IT into one of its primary activities, which also should follow and apply all the Lean principles that we have been discussing with respect to a business organization.

References

1. Womack, J., and D. Jones. 2003. *Lean thinking: Banish waste and create wealth in your corporation.* New York: Free Press.
2. Shingo, S. 1981. *A study of the Toyota Production System from an industrial engineering viewpoint.* Tokyo: Japan Management Association.

FROM BUSINESS STRATEGY TO IT ROADMAP: AN INTRODUCTION TO ENTERPRISE ARCHITECTURE (EA)

Now that we have gone through a review of key strategy concepts and business strategy formulation as well as an introduction to Lean concepts, let us now see how we can leverage these to build a Lean and Agile business organization, IT, and IT roadmap that can make a strategic contribution to the overall organization.

Chapter 4

An Introduction to Business Strategy and IT Alignment

4.1 Chapter Objective

This chapter first introduces you to the reasons why IT has not always been well-aligned with an organization's business strategy. Then, we will show why such reasons are untenable and reveal how we can leverage an IT concept called enterprise architecture (EA) to build a bridge between the business and IT worlds, in order to create a more business strategy-driven IT roadmap.

4.2 Why Business and IT Misalignment Is Unacceptable

There are a plethora of reasons why such a misalignment is unacceptable, but some of these reasons particularly stand out:

1. Despite all of the benefits that technologies and, especially, information technologies have brought about in today's world, there is nothing more wasteful than if, at the same time, a considerable amount of money is being spent to pay for this technology, especially within a given organization.
2. The high cost of spending in IT is being denied to the other departments for their needs of resources, including even IT resources.

3. The organization lacks opportunities to use the same money spent on IT on something else instead.

4. Ultimately, the organization may fail, due to the lack of effectiveness of IT and the IT department.

4.3 How Can We Identify if There Is Such Misalignment?

Whenever you observe some of the following symptoms, you will know that there is a clear misalignment between the business and IT:

1. There is no clear answer when asked how much IT is specifically contributing to the organization's business strategy (or social purpose, in the case of a nonprofit) and its bottom line.

2. Customers, as well as employees, complain about how difficult it is to use IT.

3. Most of the business units or departments within the organization have their own IT department or team.

4. There is so much overlapping or redundancy among the different IT systems that it is very difficult and costly to modify any system for a specific unit without everyone else being impacted.

5. The enterprise data reporting often results in errors and inconsistencies.

4.4 Why Has IT Never Been Clearly Aligned with the Organization's Business Strategy?

Before we begin this exciting journey, let us discuss some of the reasons why many companies, surprisingly, have not clearly aligned IT with their organization's business strategy, as depicted in Figure 4.1.

While it may sound strange to learn that an IT department's work may not be aligned with its respective organization's business strategy, it is unfortunately something we have seen too often throughout our careers.

As you may imagine, there are a variety of reasons for this situation, but several of them stand out:

1. As an organization grows, IT grows with it. However, because IT is often busy taking care of urgent problems and issues, no one feels they have the time or the need to clearly identify an organization's business strategy and the IT roadmap to support it.

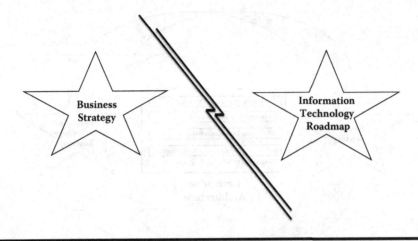

Figure 4.1 From business strategy to an IT roadmap—misalignment.

2. Of the business executives served by the IT department, whoever has the most clout or power will ultimately get served by IT first (a commonplace and well-known practice within many corporations).
3. The tenure of a CIO (Chief Information Officer) is rather short. This is why CIOs typically do not have enough time or even enough incentive to go through the exercise of building an IT roadmap for their organization.
4. There is not enough practical knowledge on the IT side to know how to identify an organization's business strategy, nor is there enough technology knowledge on the business side to know how the two sides could ultimately create an IT roadmap (let alone a Lean and Agile IT roadmap) that aligns with the organization's business strategy.

Whatever the reason, it is unacceptable when IT does not clearly support an entire organization's strategy, especially given the cost that the organization normally bears for IT and the little value IT consequently may bring to the organization's customers or constituents.

It is our hope with this book that we will enable technology leaders and business executives to understand one another and work together toward a more strategic IT for business value and innovation.

4.5 How Can We More Clearly Align IT with an Organization's Business Strategy?

As depicted in Figure 4.2, a concept known as *enterprise architecture* can be utilized to build a bridge between an organization's strategy and its technology capability.

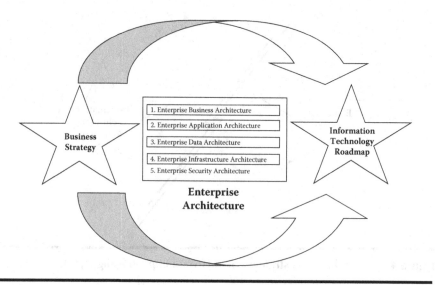

Figure 4.2 From business strategy to an IT roadmap.

4.6 Introduction to Enterprise Architecture

While there may be several definitions of EA, we consider it to be a set of artifacts and processes used to translate an organization's business strategy into an IT road-map; this will help make the organization's business strategy happen, especially if it is properly executed.

Depending on whom you ask, different practitioners may have other definitions of enterprise architecture, but, in general, it is composed of:

1. Enterprise business architecture
2. Enterprise IT application architecture
3. Enterprise IT data architecture
4. Enterprise IT infrastructure architecture
5. Enterprise security architecture

4.7 A Look at the Different Layers of an Enterprise Architecture

Let us delve into these layers, one by one, in order to better understand what comprises each layer.

1. **Enterprise business architecture**: This layer is composed of a set of business goals, business processes, and team organization. From our experience, what happens in this layer, as part of the creation of a business plan or IT roadmap, will determine what IT applications should be built to support the organization's business strategy.
2. **Enterprise IT application architecture**: This layer is composed of a set of IT applications used by teams within a commercial organization or nonprofit association to carry out its business goals and operations.
3. **Enterprise IT data architecture**: This layer is composed of a set of databases that supports an organization's core business in terms of IT applications, both transactional and analytical.
4. **Enterprise IT infrastructure architecture**: This layer of the enterprise architecture (EA) is where we can find all the hardware and servers that support an organization's IT.
5. **Enterprise security architecture**: Due to the emerging yet very important role of the Internet, we have split the work around security into a distinct layer, rather than considering it a part of the IT infrastructure layer. (For simplification, however, we will not delve into more details about this layer in the text or in the two case studies.)

4.8 Takeaways

There are many reasons why currently many IT departments' plans and activities are not supporting an organization's overall business strategy. One way to recognize if the IT department's work is not fully aligned with the organization's overall business strategy is when it is not clearly evident how much IT contributes to the organization's business or bottom line. Another way to recognize this misalignment is if many of the organization's business units have hired some of their own IT specialists to work directly under their authority. Regardless of the reason, it is not desirable or sustainable to have such a misalignment linger for a long time.

One of the best ways to create this alignment is by leveraging a concept known as enterprise architecture (EA), which, at a high level, consists of the following layers:

1. Enterprise business architecture
2. Enterprise IT application architecture
3. Enterprise IT data architecture
4. Enterprise IT infrastructure architecture
5. Enterprise security architecture

Chapter 5

More on Enterprise Architecture (EA)

5.1 Chapter Objective

While the previous chapter provided a short introduction to the concept of enterprise architecture (EA), this chapter takes a more detailed look at the different layers of the EA, examining how they fit together as part of the overall framework.

5.2 EA Framework

While there are many EA frameworks, defined as how some of these EA layers should fit together (such as the Open Group's TOGAF and the Zachmann's framework), what we are going to examine is close to the Federal Enterprise Architecture (FEA) as seen in Figure 5.1.

By further examining Figure 5.1, you can see that there are five layers to the EA.

1. Enterprise business architecture
2. Enterprise IT application architecture
3. Enterprise IT data architecture
4. Enterprise IT infrastructure architecture
5. Enterprise security architecture

In the following sections, we will review these layers, one by one, in more detail.

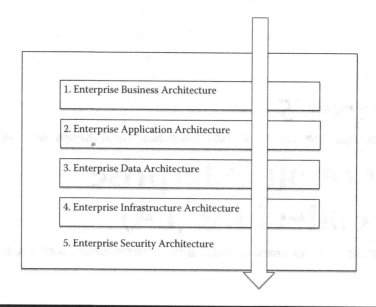

Figure 5.1   The different layers of an enterprise architecture.

5.2.1 Enterprise Business Architecture

What does the concept of enterprise business architecture mean and encompass? For the purpose of this book, we will consider this layer to be composed of:

- Business objectives, goals, and metrics
- Business processes
- Team structure

5.2.1.1 Business Objectives, Goals, and Metrics

Depending on the organization's new business strategy (as discussed in Chapters 1 and 2), examples of business objectives could include aiming to be "the first-tier player in the semiconductor business" or striving to have "the largest market share in the frozen food segment within the next two years."

While objectives are somewhat high-level, the goals used to achieve such objectives tend to be more specific and detailed in order to be implementable. For example, a goal could be to "increase sales by 5% during Q1 of next year" or "reduce inventory level for semiproducts by 10% within the next three months." Other examples of business goals are detailed in Figure 5.2.

In order to know to what extent goals have been achieved, some measurements should be identified. For the two aforementioned goals, respective examples of

Business Goals Projections

Items	Base Year	Year 1	Year 2	Year 3
Annual revenue growth rate	12%	14%	16%	18%
Revenue	$14,000,000	$15,960,000	$18,513,600	$21,846,048
Cost of goods sold (as % of revenue)	50%	50%	50%	50%
Cost of goods sold	–$7,000,000	–$7,980,000	–$9,256,800	–$10,923,024
Sales & marketing expenses (as % of revenue)	8%	10%	10%	10%
General & administrative expenses (as % of revenue)	6%	8%	8%	8%
Depreciation expenses	–$200,000	–$200,000	–$200,000	–$200,000
Tax rate	35%	35%	35%	35%

Figure 5.2   Other examples of business goals.

metrics could be "order total amounts" and the "level of inventory of semiproduct (in our SAP software system)."

5.2.1.2 Business Processes

A business process, or a workflow, is what an organization will carry out in order to fulfill its business objectives and goals.

Before we get into more details on business processes, let us say upfront that there are two types of business processes: (1) functional business processes and (2) enterprise business processes. These are shown in Figure 5.3.

By functional business processes, we refer to a business process that is only needed by a team or department within a commercial organization or nonprofit association to carry out its own activities.

By enterprise business processes, which will be the main focus of our book, we refer to a business process that originates from the customer's (or constituent's) or supplier's side. These enterprise business processes constitute an organization's value streams, especially the ones that relate directly to the customers' needs.

Because this book focuses on Lean and Agile IT, we will focus on the enterprise business processes that are geared toward meeting the organization's customer value.

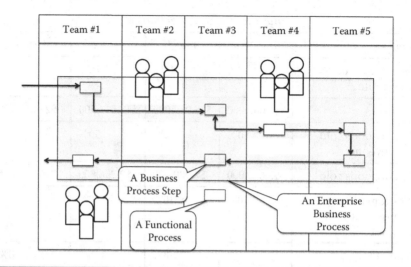

Figure 5.3 A business's functional and enterprise processes.

As we will demonstrate later, the majority of these processes can be drilled down to greater levels of detail, allowing us to have a better idea of what specific activities the teams will need to carry out. This is especially key as we attempt to avoid the duplication of IT systems.

As demonstrated in Figure 5.4, a process can encompass many steps.

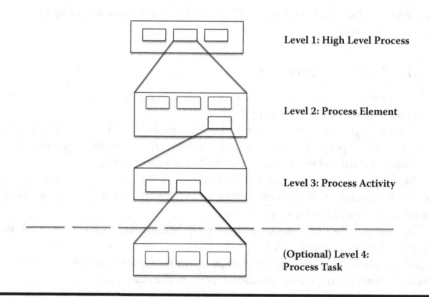

Figure 5.4 Different levels of detail of an enterprise process.

Because we advocate a Lean and Agile organization (and a Lean and Agile IT), we next will go through a technique called the *Ishikawa diagram*, which we can use to identify these enterprise business processes, before we look at another technique we can use to streamline these processes called business process value modeling.

5.2.1.2.1 Ishikawa Diagramming Technique

The Ishikawa diagramming technique can be used to (1) determine major causes of a phenomenon, (2) determine potential root causes of a problem, (3) identify solutions to an identified problem, or (4) optimize a process.

Below is how you can draw an Ishikawa diagram, otherwise known as a Fishbone diagram.

- First, start by briefly naming the problem or issue you want to resolve at the end of the diagram.
- Next, identify the different categories of what could be the solutions or causes.
- Then, brainstorm with the rest of the team to look for causes within the different categories.

For illustrative purposes, Figure 5.5 and Figure 5.6 convey an example of an Ishikawa diagram and a resulting enterprise business process, respectively.

5.2.1.2.2 Business Process Value Modeling

Assume now that Figure 5.6 is our current order fulfillment enterprise business process, but it is not very satisfactory. Let us go through an exercise of business process

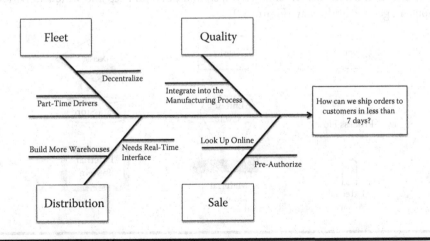

Figure 5.5   The Ishikawa diagramming technique.

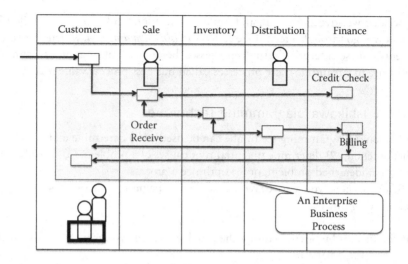

Figure 5.6 Enterprise business process.

value modeling to see how we might eventually take some of the noncustomer-value added activities out of the flow.

To begin, let us first examine Figure 5.7, which contains all of the symbols that we are going to utilize for the next step.

Now assume that you have used some of the symbols in Figure 5.7 to create one of your business processes or customer value streams. What you obtain will look like Figure 5.8 for what may be called a customer order fulfillment enterprise business process.

Before you optimize your business processes, let us look at the different types of activities and determine which ones you should or could keep and which activities you can get out of the way (Figure 5.9).

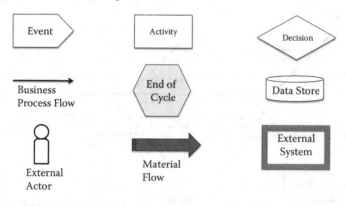

Figure 5.7 Symbols used in business process value modeling.

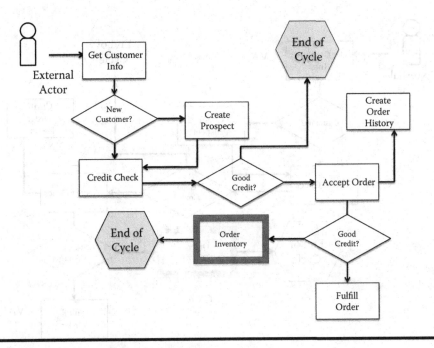

Figure 5.8   Business process modeling.

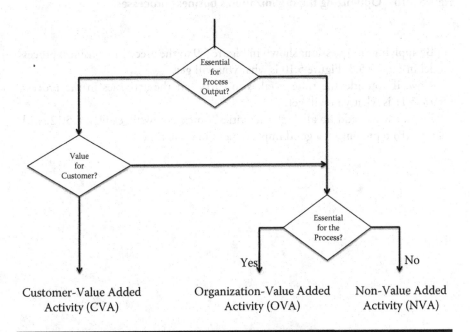

Figure 5.9   Is your activity customer-value added or not?

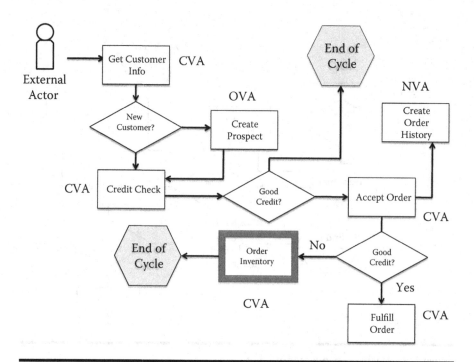

Figure 5.10 Optimizing the organization's business processes.

By applying the questions shown in Figure 5.9 to the preceding business process model in Figure 5.8, Figure 5.10 is what you will get.

Now, if you add the time it takes to carry out the activities in the process, Figure 5.11 is what you will get.

Finally, if you add up all of the activities' times, you will get Figure 5.12, with column (B) representing a good improvement in cycle time.

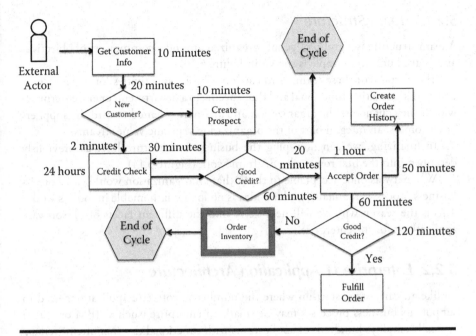

Figure 5.11 Calculating the process cycle time.

Process Activities	Current Cycle Time (A)	Optimized Cycle Time (B)
Step #1	10 minutes	5 minutes
Step #2	20 minutes	4 minutes
Step #3	10 minutes	2 minutes
Step #n	n minutes	n minutes
Total	476 minutes	315 minutes

Figure 5.12 Adding up all the activities' times.

5.2.1.3 Team Structure

A team structure is a group of people organized around a common set of objectives and goals. Such an example is shown in Figure 5.13.

The purpose of these teams is to carry out business activities (or business processes) that are either functional and thus specific to a department, or else enterprise-wide if they cut across the organization and are more oriented toward the suppliers or customers, an integral part of the organization's specific value streams.

In finalizing, we can now plug the business architecture layer as previously described into the first row of the EA framework (Figure 5.14).

While it was once acceptable to think that an organization would carry out its business processes manually, such an idea is no longer fathomable in today's world. This is the reason why we will next delve into the different facets of IT software applications for the enterprise.

5.2.2 Enterprise IT Application Architecture

Unlike an early-stage start-up where the number of software applications used to support its business processes may be small, an enterprise (such as IBM or Cisco) typically employs hundreds of applications with functionalities that often overlap.

An example of enterprise IT application architecture is shown at the second level of Figure 5.15.

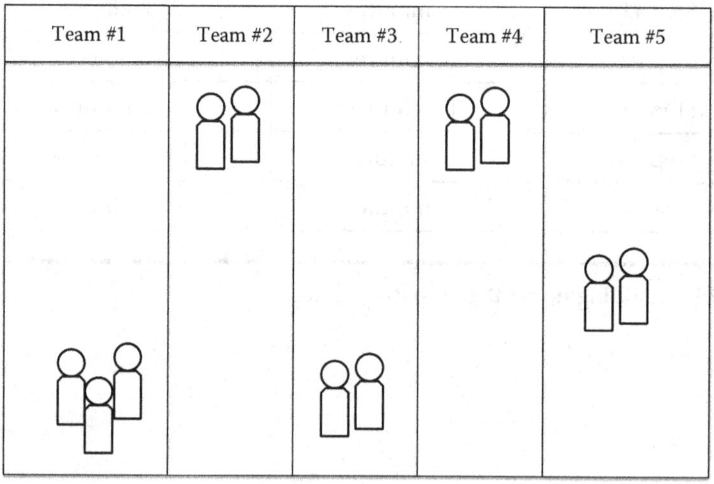

Figure 5.13 An example of team structure.

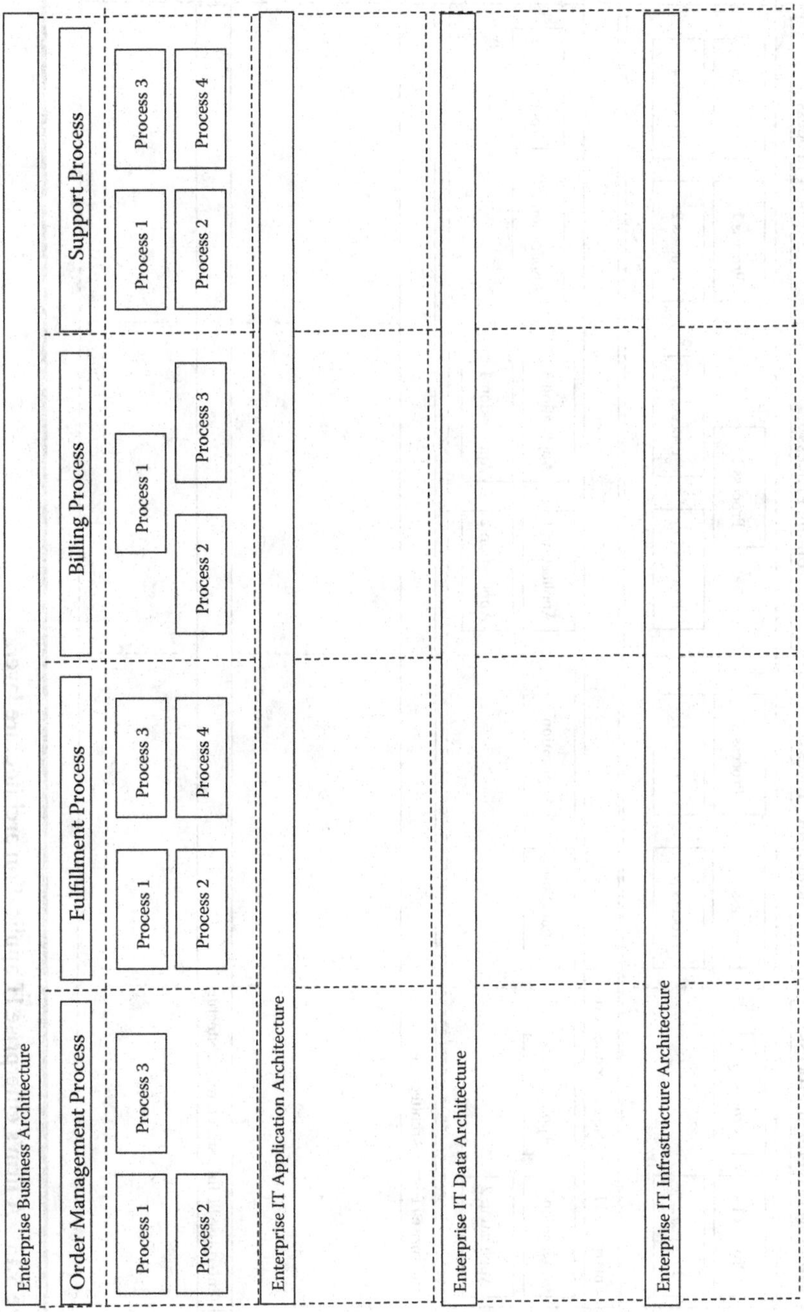

Figure 5.14   A firm's enterprise business process layer.

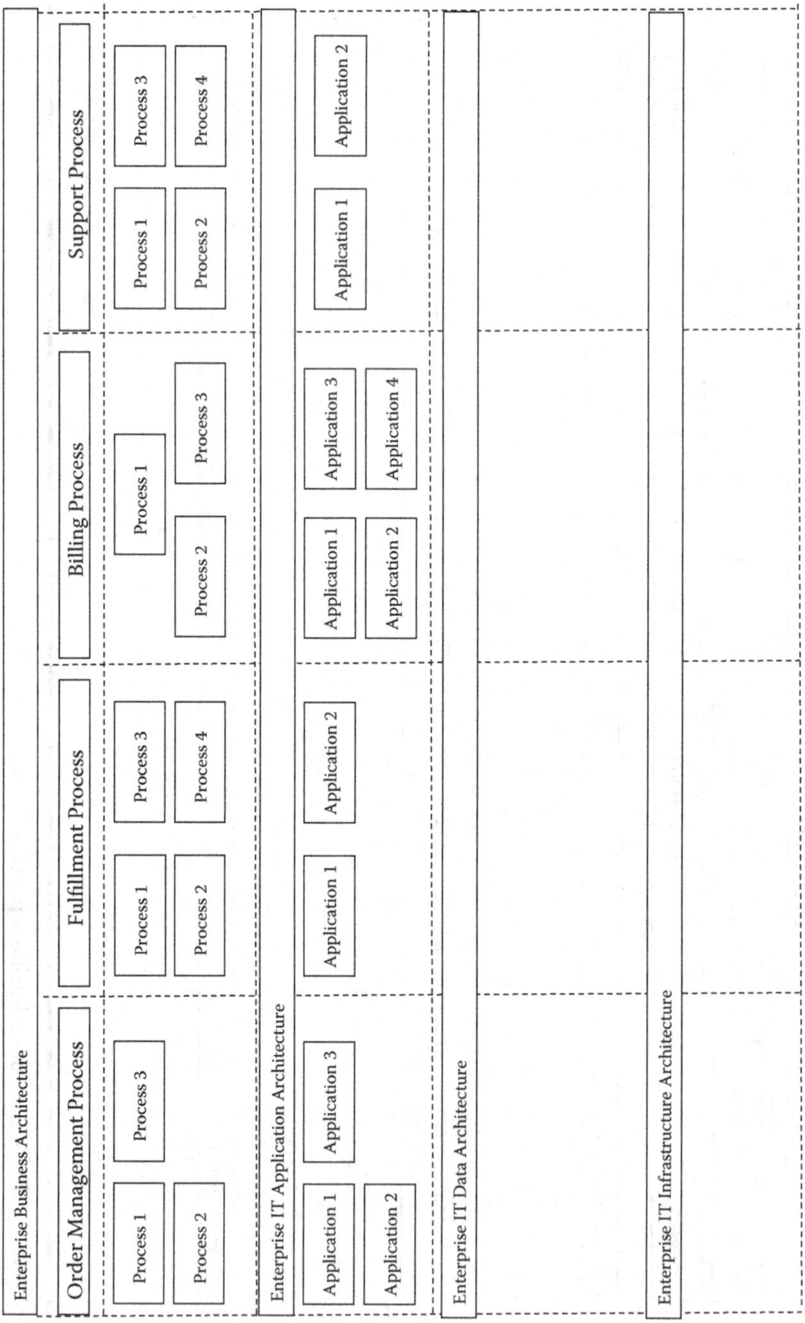

Figure 5.15 A firm's enterprise IT application architecture layer.

5.2.3 *Enterprise IT Data Architecture*

Since every application has to manipulate a small or large database in the backend, you can imagine the number of databases with which an organization has to deal. Unless these databases have been well architected or organized, an organization may end up having to deal with a maze of databases with potential redundancies, resulting in countless contradictions and sleepless nights for the organization's CFO (Chief Financial Officer).

An example of databases and IT data architecture is shown at the third level of Figure 5.16. Though we will deal with this subject in greater detail, for now, let us say that there are two types of IT data architecture: transactional and data warehousing.

5.2.4 *Enterprise IT Infrastructure Architecture*

Next, there is the enterprise IT infrastructure layer where all of the enterprise's hardware and servers are located, as depicted at the bottom of Figure 5.17.

Despite the fact that strategic misalignment rarely originates from this layer of the enterprise architecture, disregarding this layer, especially given the current IT situation within most organizations, can very much hurt their agility and ability to compete.

Providing proof of how key it is to have a well-aligned enterprise IT architecture supported by a well-integrated IT infrastructure, it is interesting to note, as reported by the *Wall Street Journal* 2012 article, that the Chinese PC maker Lenovo had been unable to fully benefit from its acquisition of IBM's PC business unit, based on the thousands of nonintegrated applications, due to the old IBM PC business unit's enterprise IT infrastructure. This hindrance lasted until Lenovo, finally, successfully upgraded the antiquated IBM's IT infrastructure and seamlessly integrated it into Lenovo's new overall IT infrastructure.[1]

At the same time, as we will see when discussing future enterprise infrastructure, because these servers can cost tens of millions of dollars (especially if their growth is overly complex and cannot be easily contained), it is more and more in the interest of organizations to either outsource the support for this IT infrastructure to specialized firms or to make the move to cloud computing, once the organization has been successful in simplifying and re-aligning the IT infrastructure with the organization's business strategy.

The above being said, for organizations that feel it is better for them to retain direct control of this layer, it is important to note that the industry trend, for the past few years, has not been to place emphasis on what types of advanced technologies organizations should have in the data center, but to assess how much these technologies can really help support and grow the business's strategy and bottom line.[1]

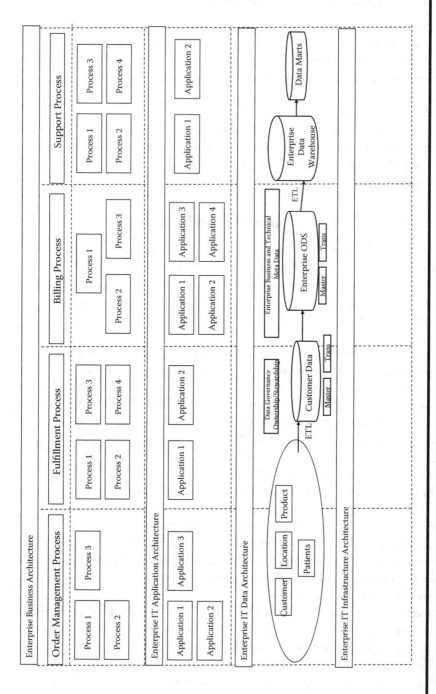

Figure 5.16 A firm's enterprise IT data architecture layer.

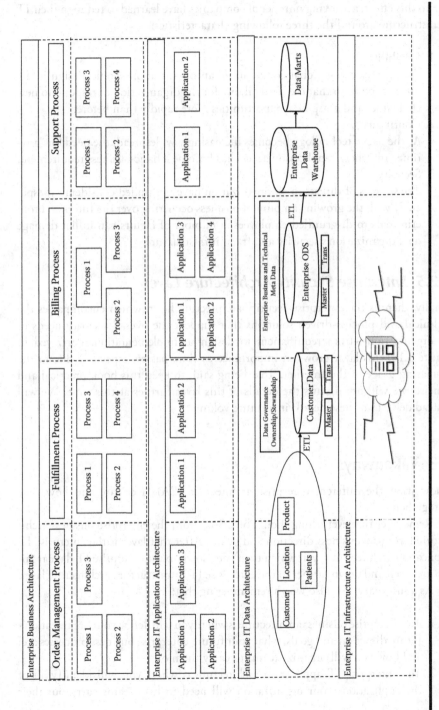

Figure 5.17 A firm's enterprise IT infrastructure architecture layer.

To this effect, a growing number of companies have learned to redesign their IT infrastructure around the three following characteristics:

1. Flexibility
   Facing increasing global competition, an organization should design its IT infrastructure so that the result allows for the organization to respond to new challenges and grasp new opportunities more rapidly than before.
2. Continuity
   As the use of technology becomes increasingly widespread, the need for "anytime, anywhere" application access has become a basic business requirement.
3. Security
   The sources of threats to an organization have multiplied considerably, especially with the growing amount of business occurring over the Internet. From criminals to disgruntled employees, a number of factors can inflict damage on a organization's security and fraud infrastructure.

5.2.5 Enterprise Security Architecture Layer

Finally, there is the enterprise security architecture layer, which encompasses the technical and process-driven solutions that support the overall security needs of an organization—from requirement to design to implementation. Portrayed in Figure 5.18, this layer grows in importance as time passes, especially due to the increasing usage of the Internet. That being said, to keep this book practical and concise, we will not discuss the details of this layer further at this time. We will instead delve into these details in a future volume.

5.3 Takeaways

Know what the different enterprise architecture (EA) layers are and how they fit together.

Remember that everything should be driven from the enterprise business architecture layer (the business direction and goals). After that layer is the enterprise IT application architecture layer, which then goes down to the enterprise IT data architecture layer, and down farther to the enterprise IT infrastructure architecture layer.

As a summary, it is also worth remembering that:

1. The enterprise business architecture is where you will define your organization's future direction and goals; what your future enterprise business processes are; and how you will organize teams to carry them out.
2. The enterprise IT application architecture is where you will identify all of the applications your organization will need to help teams carry out their

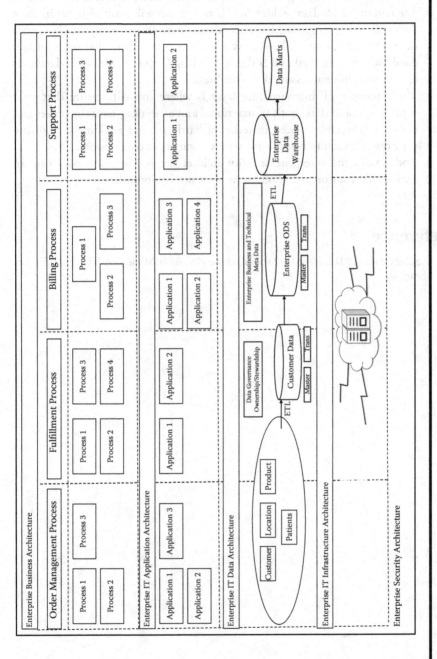

Figure 5.18 A firm's enterprise security architecture layer.

processes. It is also where you will identify how they should interact with one another to allow your organization to better serve its customers or constituents.

3. The enterprise IT data architecture is where you will want to organize how data will be structured, such that no data can be created or updated by more than one application. Likewise, you will want to ensure that some master databases are identified and laid down to help keep the number of databases low while helping to assure data consistency.

4. The enterprise IT infrastructure layer is where you will ensure that your applications and data, both transactional and analytical, have the power and flexibility they might need in terms of hardware and equipment, allowing your organization to better serve your customers or constituents.

5. And finally, the enterprise security architecture is where you will want to ensure that your organization's security is not compromised.

Reference

1. Schectman, J. 2012. How Lenovo pulled the plug on IBM's legacy, *Wall Street Journal.* August 7.

FROM BUSINESS STRATEGY TO AN AGILE AND LEAN IT ROADMAP: THE FORMULATION PROCESS

IV

Now that we have gone through a high level review of the different enterprise architecture (EA) layers, let us see how we can utilize them to build an IT road-map, as can be seen in Figure 6.1. Our intent in providing a high-level formulation process overview is to provide you with an opportunity to pause and reflect on what you have seen in terms of business strategy before we next delve into the details of the IT roadmap formulation in Chapter 7.

Chapter 6

A High-Level Overview of the IT Roadmap Formulation Process

6.1 Chapter Objective

This chapter walks you through the different steps in the process of creating and aligning the IT roadmap, whether in support of a for-profit or nonprofit organization's business strategy.

6.2 Step 1: Identify Current Business and IT Situation

As a first step, take a snapshot of the current situation of the organization, both in terms of business and IT.

On the business side, this means identifying the current enterprise business architecture, that is, the current business goals, business processes, and team structure.

On the IT side, this means identifying the current enterprise IT application architecture, the current enterprise IT data architecture, and the current enterprise IT infrastructure architecture.

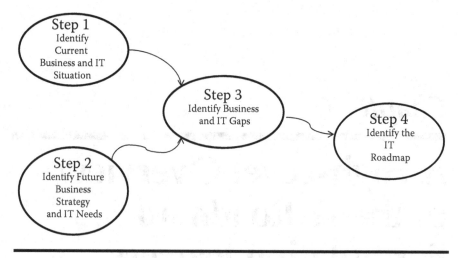

Figure 6.1   A high-level overview of the roadmap formulation process.

6.3 Step 2: Identify Future Business Strategy and IT Needs

As discussed in both Chapter 1 and 2, this is when an effort should be made to identify the organization's future business strategy and business direction.

Once you know more about your organization's future business direction and financial goals, you should proceed to identify what this means in terms of the future enterprise business architecture. In other words, you should identify business goals, future business processes, and future team organization.

On the IT side, you should proceed to identify the future applications, data, and infrastructure architecture that will be needed to support this new business strategy.

Even though we mention this step after the identification of the current business and IT situation, this does not mean that you cannot start the IT roadmap formulation process by identifying the new business strategy and IT needs first. To the contrary, doing this also could help you and your executive teams be more creative and innovative by abstracting what you know about the current business and IT situation.

6.4 Step 3: Identify Business and IT Gaps

Following the two steps above, you should next evaluate the current IT situation against this new business strategy to form a better idea of how well the current IT applications, data, and infrastructure support the future business strategy.

Armed with the results from the two previous steps, lay the future IT needs over the current IT artifacts to identify the gaps that should be part of the IT roadmap.

In short, now is the time to attempt to identify gaps (1) in enterprise business processes, (2) in enterprise IT application architecture, (3) in enterprise IT data architecture, and (4) in enterprise IT infrastructure architecture. All of these gaps, when combined, will form what we will call an IT roadmap. However, to clarify our purpose, an IT roadmap does not have to only contain investment toward new in-house software development alone. It also should sometimes, if not more often, include the acquisition of commercial off-the-shelf (COTS) software as well.

6.5 Step 4: Identify the IT Roadmap

By laying the future IT needs derived from the new business directions over the current IT artifacts and identifying the resulting gaps, we will be able to derive the new business processes, applications, data, and infrastructure needed to create the new IT roadmap. By knowing what artifacts will be needed, we will be able to also identify the financial and human resources needed to support the execution of the new IT roadmap.

6.6 Takeaways

Whether you start by identifying the current IT situation or the future business strategy first, you should make sure that your organization's future business direction and goals drive the creation of an IT roadmap.

If you happen to be a start-up or new organization without much historical baggage, you do not always have to first take a formal snapshot of the current business and IT situation. Instead, what you should do is identify the organization's new business strategy and direction before you lay the organization's future IT needs over the current IT situation and derive the IT roadmap from there.

Chapter 7

More on the IT Roadmap Formulation Process

7.1 Chapter Objective

The intent of this chapter is to walk the reader through the granular details behind the formulation process of an IT roadmap, examining the different detailed steps that need to be carried out. We will first look at each step, including what each means conceptually, and next look at how to carry out these steps in the trenches (Figure 7.1).

7.2 Step 1: Identify the Current Business and IT Situation

7.2.1 Current Enterprise Business Architecture

As previously mentioned, there are at least three things that will need to be completed at this level:

1. Business goals and metrics
2. Business processes
3. Team structure

Before we expand on the discussion, here is a brief review of each requirement:

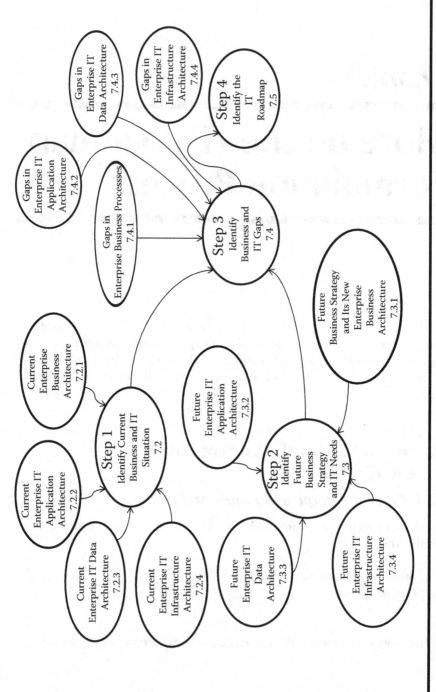

Figure 7.1 Detailed IT roadmap elaboration process.

7.2.1.1 Business Goals and Metrics

Examples of business goals include establishing targets, such as "to increase sales by 5% during Q1 of next year" or "to reduce inventory level for semiproducts by 10% within the next three months."

Metrics, meanwhile, are the measurements by which we determine whether business goals have been reached. For example, metrics for the two aforementioned goals could be "total order amounts" and the "level of inventory of semiproducts (in the organization's SAP software system)," respectively.

Before we move into the business process aspect of the enterprise business architecture layer, let us briefly remind ourselves what a *core competency* is. As mentioned in Chapter 2, a core competency is a key capability that is central to the very foundation of a business and to the way it operates. For example, L'Oréal's core competency is the knowledge that forms the very root of the beauty products and processes that L'Oréal puts in place in order to offer women and men worldwide the best of cosmetics innovation with respect to quality, efficacy, and safety.

As such, the role of an organization is to perform all of the tasks or activities that have deep roots in its core competency, in order to differentiate itself from its competitors.

7.2.1.2 Business Processes

As mentioned before, let us briefly restate that there are two types of business processes:

1. Functional business processes
2. Enterprise business processes

7.2.1.2.1 Functional Business Processes

As shown in Figure 7.2, the business processes that a business unit carries out for its own work are referred to as functional business processes.

Though the business processes in Figure 7.2 appear rather simple, it is only because we observe them from a high level. Otherwise, a functional business process can be broken down further into much greater detail, as shown in Figure 7.3.

7.2.1.2.2 Enterprise Business Processes

As mentioned in Chapter 2, the second type of business process is an enterprise business process. Before we get deeper into this, let us pinpoint the main difference between a functional process and an enterprise process: while a functional process serves only one team and its result is only for that particular team, an enterprise business process cuts across multiple teams within an organization and always originates from either the customer or the supplier (Figure 7.4).

Your Enterprise or Business Unit

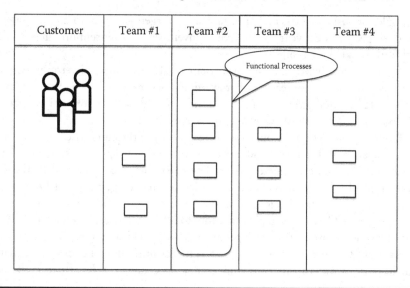

Figure 7.2 Functional business processes.

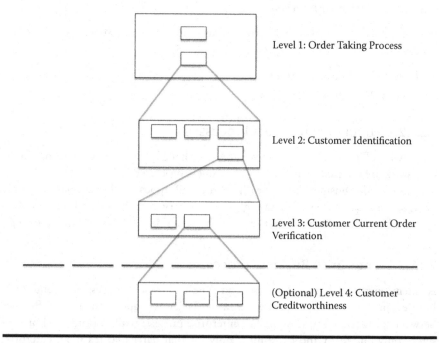

Figure 7.3 Decomposition of a functional business process.

Your Enterprise or Business Unit

Customer	Team #1	Team #2	Team #3	Team #4

Enterprise Business Process

Figure 7.4   Example of enterprise business processes.

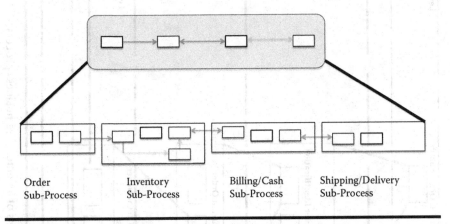

| Order Sub-Process | Inventory Sub-Process | Billing/Cash Sub-Process | Shipping/Delivery Sub-Process |

Figure 7.5   Different components of an enterprise business process.

Similar to the decomposition of the functional business process observed in Figure 7.3, an enterprise business process also can be broken down into further detail, as shown in Figure 7.5.

Meanwhile, Figure 7.5 can be broken down into still greater detail, as shown in Figure 7.6.

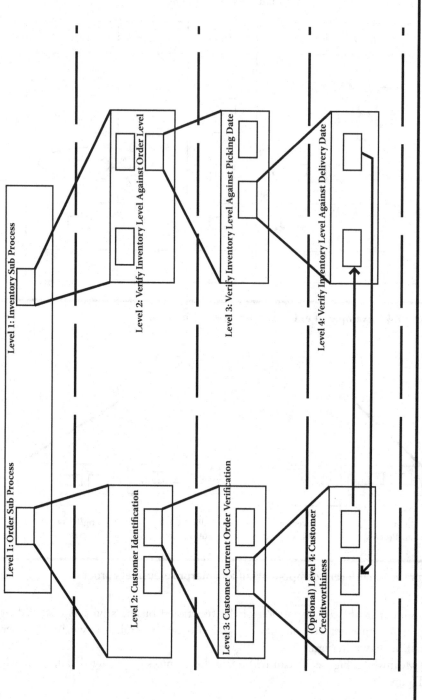

Figure 7.6 Detailed levels of an enterprise business process.

In the same way that there are two types of business processes, there are also two types of enterprise business processes: (1) customer-facing enterprise business processes and (2) supplier-facing enterprise business processes.

In order to illustrate the difference between a customer-facing enterprise business process and a supplier-facing enterprise business process, Figure 7.7 offers an example of the customer-facing enterprise processes (that take care of customer needs), while Figure 7.8 provides an example of the supplier-facing enterprise business processes (that deal with the supplier side).

7.2.1.3 Team Structure

Normally, we would not provide suggestions on how a business should organize its teams. However, because our approach involves building a Lean and Agile organization and IT, we will instead recommend that you keep the big picture in mind when organizing teams, in order to avoid duplication or the creation of nonvalue-added activities that have been plaguing organizations of all kinds to this day (Figure 7.9).

Next, as our discussion is about Lean enterprise business processes, it is important to know how your business unit will fit into the overall enterprise structure, as shown in Figure 7.10.

In order to recap and create an overview of all the enterprise business processes and the different team participants involved, you could organize these components into a table like the one shown in Figure 7.11. Using this method, you would be able to see what teams might become overloaded and if there is an opportunity to consolidate or distribute work such that things would become more balanced. For example, in Figure 7.11, it is apparent that Team #2 is overloaded.

7.2.2 Current Enterprise IT Application Architecture

Once the current business processes have been studied, or in parallel with the study of the business process, the next, or other, step is to take a snapshot of the current enterprise's IT application architecture, as shown in Figure 7.12.

The goal of having a snapshot of the current IT applications is not only to know what they are, but also to assess their fit into the future needs of the organization. This is why it will be not only important to study these applications' strength and weaknesses in themselves, as in Figure 7.14, but be equally essential to study the different interfaces between these applications (Figure 7.13).

Lastly, in order to complete the current IT assessment, we should finally analyze each of the applications in terms of their business alignment, maintainability, architecture, modularity, and scalability, as shown in Figure 7.14.

In this assessment, we can easily envision, for instance, that any application that scores less than 2.5 in business alignment or in total average score should be decommissioned or retired.

Enterprise Business Processes \ Process Characteristic	Name of Process	Customer	Team #1, #2, Etc.	Suppliers
Enterprise Process #1	Order to Cash	X	X	X
	Order to Make	X	X	
Enterprise Process #2	Order to Ship			
	Order to Store			
Enterprise Process #3				

Figure 7.7 Customer-facing enterprise business processes.

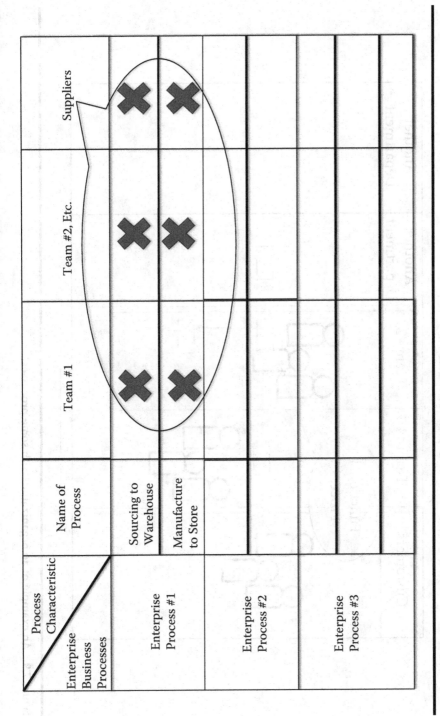

Figure 7.8 Supplier-facing enterprise business processes.

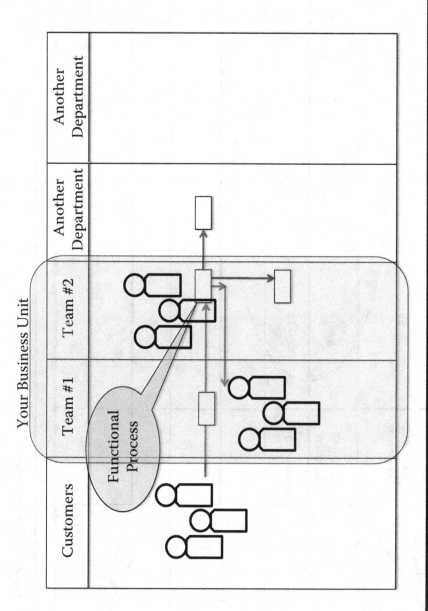

Figure 7.9 An example of an organization with some processes.

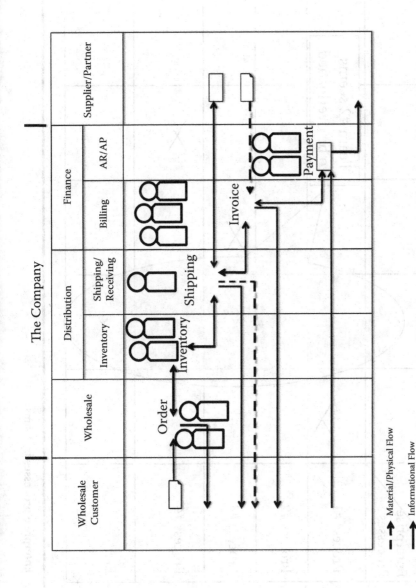

Figure 7.10 Current processes and enterprise organization.

Teams / Enterprise Processes	Team #1	Team #2	Team #3	Team #4	Etc.
Process #1	X				
Process #2		X			
Process #3		X	X		
Process #4		X		X	
Etc.		X			

Team #2 seems to be overloaded

Figure 7.11 Enterprise processes by teams.

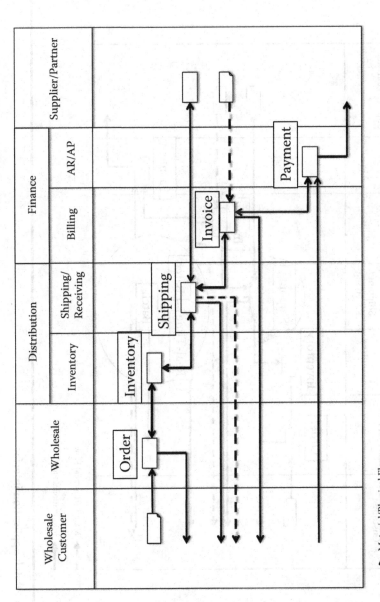

Figure 7.12   A firm's current enterprise IT application architecture.

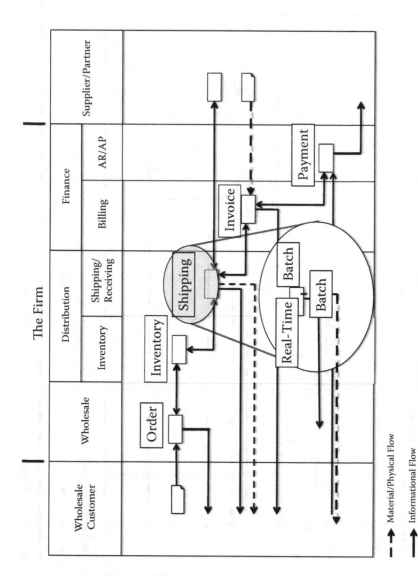

Figure 7.13 Batch application interface.

	Score					
Applications	Business Alignment	Maintainability	Architecture	Modularity	Scalability	Average Score
					Minimum: 1 Maximum: 5	
1. Order	2	3	5	4	4	3.6
2. Inventory	2	5	5	4	4	4.0
3. Shipping	2	3	3	2	1	2.2
4. Invoice	2	3	1	3	1	2.0
5. Etc.						

Figure 7.14   Current IT application architectural assessment.

Enterprise Processes	Applications				
	App #1	App #2	App #3	App # 4	Etc.
Process #1	x				
Process #2		x			
Process #3		x	x		
Process #4		x		x	
Etc.		x			

Figure 7.15   Enterprise processes by teams.

In order to complete the above application assessment, it will also be crucial to examine how the current enterprise business processes would be supported by these applications (Figure 7.15).

From Figure 7.15, it appears as though application #2 is the most important application that the organization relies on. Knowing this should lead to the realization that either greater investment is required to renovate the application or that the application should be replaced if the current version is too old or costly to be renovated.

It is also important to examine, at the same time that this analysis is being carried out, how the different processes are being rather taken care of and by which teams.

From Figure 7.16, we can see that there is a rather balanced allocation of workflow and responsibility between the different teams.

Enterprise Processes	Applications				
	App #1	App #2	App #3	App #4	Etc.
Process #1	x				
Process #2		x			
Process #3			x		
Process #4	x			x	x
Etc.					

Figure 7.16   Enterprise processes by teams.

7.2.3 Current Enterprise IT Data Architecture

In the same way that we assessed the current IT applications and gauged their strengths and weaknesses, we should assess as well the current enterprise IT data architecture. More often than not, data can pose even more concerns and issues than IT applications, especially when it comes to financial reporting and regulation.

Like many things we have previously reviewed, there are two types of enterprise IT data architecture: enterprise IT transactional data architecture and enterprise IT business intelligence data architecture.

7.2.3.1 Enterprise IT Transactional Data Architecture

An issue often encountered with enterprise transactional IT data architecture is that the same data is often created or updated by multiple applications. As a result, it can be very difficult to know which application updated what data the last time and to which business unit this application belongs.

As shown in Figure 7.17, data entity #1 seems to be updated by not only application #2 but also by applications #3 and #4. At the same time, data entity #2 could not only be created and deleted by application #2 but also by application #4, which can create a lot of confusion since we may not know which of the two applications would have deleted data entity #2.

7.2.3.2 Enterprise IT Business Intelligence Data Architecture

More often than not, the situation can be even worse in enterprise business intelligence (BI) IT data architecture. This leads us, very often, to hear that the same data

Data	Current IT Applications				
	App #1	*App #2*	*App #3*	*App #4*	*Etc.*
Data entity #1	C	U	U	U	
Data entity #2		C/U/D		C/D	
Data entity #3		C	R	U	
Data entity #4	U	U	U		
Etc.					

Note: C = Create; U = Update; D = Delete; R = Read.

Figure 7.17   Data by current IT applications.

fields' values in different business units' reports do not even match one another. One of the reasons why this might occur is because many transactional applications may be updating the same data fields' values, which are accessed or retrieved at different times by different departments.

Another potential reason for this inconsistency is due to the fact that there is (1) no master data nor (2) a good BI data architecture. For the former, that often leads to the multiplication of databases that can come into conflict with one another. For the latter, that often means that sometimes the data pulled into different reports may come from the data feeds that are not part of the Enterprise Data Warehouse (EDW).

As shown in Figure 7.18, this seems to be the case with report A, which pulls in data not only from the Data Warehouse, but also from "X" and "Y" data feeds.

7.2.4 Current Enterprise IT Infrastructure Architecture

Our final step will be to conduct an inventory of the organization's current IT infrastructure and analyze how many databases, routers, or servers are running the organization's software applications and whether these are adequate. As such, we will be using the results of this inventory as the baseline against the future IT infrastructure needs.

For simplicity, we can use a diagram (such as the one depicted in Figure 7.19) to conceptually model the IT infrastructure architecture, which is similar to the way in which the ISO (International Organization of Standards) seven layers are typically depicted.

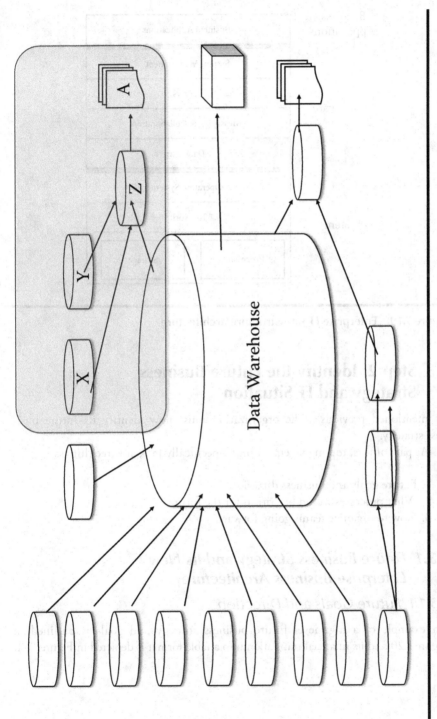

Figure 7.18 Current data warehouse architecture.

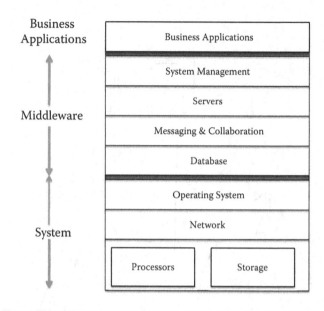

Figure 7.19   Enterprise IT infrastructure architecture.

7.3 Step 2: Identify the Future Business Strategy and IT Situation

As mentioned previously, the organization must now identify its future business strategy.

As part of this, top management must specifically look at three things:

1. Future goals and business direction
2. What processes would be critical for the future
3. How to organize teams going forward

7.3.1 Future Business Strategy and Its New Enterprise Business Architecture

7.3.1.1 Future Goals and Direction

An example of a high-level future business strategy and goals is outlined in Figure 7.20 and its financial translation into a table format is depicted in Figure 7.21.

Traditional	Organic Growth	Partnership	Acquisition
Traditional sale of semifinished and finished products	Diversify into individual markets	Partnerships in specific areas of technology	Acquire customer's operations Long-term supply chain agreement
Traditional Transactions	Diversification ⟶		Strategic Partnerships

Figure 7.20   Example of future business direction.

Business Goals Projections

Items	Base Year	Year 1	Year 2	Year 3
Annual revenue growth rate	20%	20%	25%	30%
Revenue	$30,000,000	$36,000,000	$45,000,000	$58,500,000
Cost of goods sold (as % of revenue)	20%	18%	16%	14%
Cost of goods sold	–$6,000,000	–$6,480,000	–$7,200,000	–$8,190,000
Sales & marketing expenses (as % of revenue)	15%	15%	10%	10%
General & administrative expenses (as % of revenue)	10%	10%	5%	5%
Depreciation expenses	–$300,000	–$300,000	–$300,000	–$300,000
Tax rate	35%	35%	35%	35%

Figure 7.21   Another example of business goals.

7.3.1.2 Enterprise Business Processes

In support of their future business strategy, top management should then decide, going forward, on what enterprise processes they will need to focus their future business.

For illustrative purposes, below are some examples of what management might go through when conducting enterprise processes evaluation (Figure 7.22 and Figure 7.23).

By looking at Figure 7.22, we can see that the top management of this organization seems to have identified some new customer-facing enterprise processes in processes #1 and #2, again detailed in Figure 7.23.

By looking at Figure 7.23, which we will discuss further when we talk about process gaps later on, we can see that the future enterprise process #1, which will ensure that orders are delivered on time, seems to be a signal from top management that their new focus will be to completely take care of customers' needs first, ahead of any financial concern. At the same time, enterprise process #2, as an entirely new

Enterprise Business Processes	Teams			
	Customer	Order	Distribution	Finance
Enterprise process #1	x	x	x	
Enterprise process #2	x	x		x
Etc.				

Figure 7.22   Identifying the future enterprise business processes.

Enterprise Processes	Teams			
	Customer	Order	Distribution	Finance
Current enterprise process #1	x	x		x
Future enterprise process #1	x	x	x	
Current enterprise process #2 (N/A)				
Future enterprise process #2	x	x		x

Figure 7.23   Future enterprise business processes (over the current processes).

process, shows the importance for the management team to separately and readily recognize revenue as soon as the customer places his or her order.

7.3.1.3 Team Structure

After top management has decided which new enterprise business processes they should focus on, they will need to decide how they would like to organize the teams going forward in such a way that will allow them to take care of and leverage the new enterprise business processes in an effective manner.

For example, would the organization need to centralize or decentralize its current structure? To answer such a question, the organization would need to think about whether it should keep everything in-house, outsource, or offshore a portion of its activities while keeping the other portion of its activities in-house.

7.3.2 Future Enterprise IT Application Architecture

Depending on which enterprise business processes management has decided to focus on, they will next need to select the type of IT applications which they think will best support the teams along with the new business processes, either by enhancing some of the current IT applications or by commissioning a new set of applications to be built. An example of the overall IT application architecture for the new enterprise business processes is shown in Figure 7.24.

While Figure 7.24 can be considered to be a logical or conceptual architecture, Figure 7.25 is an example of how it can be deployed physically using an architectural style that has come to be known as Service-Oriented Architecture (SOA)—based on an Enterprise Service Bus (ESB).

Whenever an organization has the opportunity to better serve its customers' or donors' value, it should try to reorganize its enterprise business processes as much as possible—while also ensuring that its IT applications are evenly balanced; that is, they should serve a cohesive grouping of enterprise business processes, as shown in Figure 7.26.

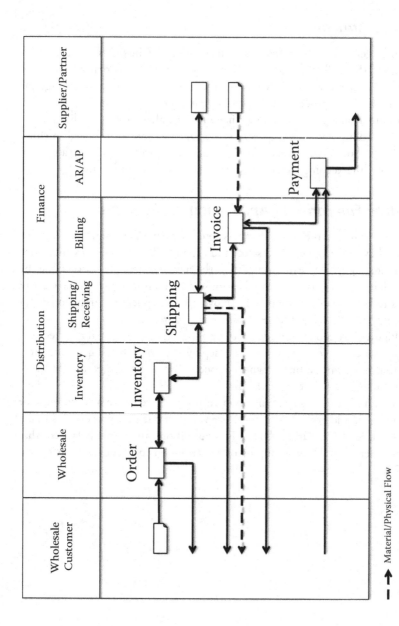

Figure 7.24   Example of future enterprise IT application architecture.

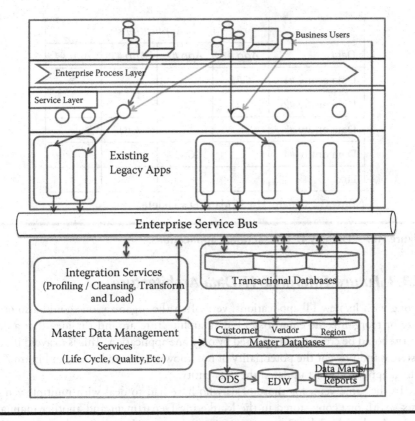

Figure 7.25   An example of service-oriented architecture (SOA).

IT Applications / New Business Processes	App #1	App #2	App #3	App #4
Process #1		x	x	x
Process #2	x			x
Process #3		x	x	
Process #4	x		x	
Etc.				

Figure 7.26   From process to application.

Data	IT Applications			
	App #1	App #2	App #3	App #4
Data entity #1	C/U			
Data entity #2		C/U	D	
Data entity #3			C/U	
Data entity #4		C/U		
Etc.				

Note: C = Create; U = Update; D = Delete.

Figure 7.27 Data by IT transactional applications.

7.3.3 Future Enterprise IT Data Architecture

Along with its new IT applications, very often the organization should also organize or reorganize its enterprise IT data architecture around the idea that a data entry should be created and updated by only one application. This is to avoid inconsistency and prevent the potentiality of not knowing, as can be seen in Figure 7.27, which application last updated the data entity.

In the same vein, for those of us who have had to deal with multiple vendor lists—with one copy stored in the Marketing Department and another manually maintained in the Sales Department—it will become obvious that the organization should also try to set up some sort of reference databases as part of a Master Data Management (MDM) layer, in order to avoid exactly this type of conflicting database multiplication.

With the MDM in place, the traditional—and often chaotic—enterprise IT data architecture, as shown in Figure 7.28, will become much more organized, looking more like Figure 7.29.

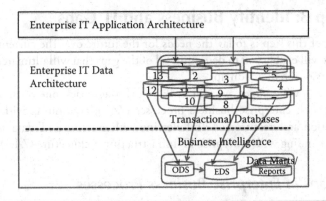

Figure 7.28   Enterprise IT data architecture without MDM.

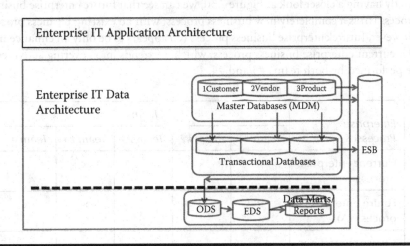

Figure 7.29   Enterprise IT data architecture with MDM.

7.3.4 Future Enterprise IT Infrastructure Architecture

In order to pursue our review of the different enterprise architecture layers, imagine that the same organization's top management has decided that, in order to better support their new business strategy, they should modernize and standardize their IT infrastructure architecture around:

1. Some more powerful servers, storage, and network upgrades;
2. Along with a gradual migration to cloud computing (which is described in more detail in Appendix E).

7.4 Step 3: Identify Business and IT Gaps

The intent of this step is to lay the needs for the future over the current situation. Doing this will enable you to determine all of the gaps that will ultimately form the components of the IT roadmap.

In the following pages, we will walk you through each one of these IT gaps, beginning with enterprise business processes (7.4.1), continuing with enterprise IT application architecture (7.4.2), following with enterprise IT data architecture (7.4.3), and ending with enterprise IT infrastructure architecture (7.4.4).

7.4.1 Gaps in Enterprise Business Processes

For illustrative purposes, Figure 7.30 shows an example of gaps in terms of future enterprise business processes over some of the existing enterprise business processes.

By having a closer look at Figure 7.30, we can see that future enterprise business process (B) is a completely new business process, with no existing business process. However, future enterprise business process (C) appears to be only an enhancement of a current enterprise business process, which it extends into covering activities to be performed by both teams #3 and #4.

Enterprise Processes	Teams				
	Team #1	Team #2	Team #3	Team #4	Team #5
Current enterprise process	×	×		×	
Future enterprise process (A)	×	×		×	×
Current enterprise process (N/A)					
Future enterprise process (B)		×	×		×
Current enterprise process	×	×			
Future enterprise process (C)	×	×	×	×	

Figure 7.30　Gaps in enterprise business processes.

7.4.2 Gaps in Enterprise IT Application Architecture

By laying the future application needs over the current IT applications, as shown in Figure 7.31, you can see that there seem to be three cases that stand out in this diagram:

1. The future enterprise business process (A) represents, along with its supporting IT applications, an enhancement of the current enterprise business process by extending its coverage over to customer service (which is provided by an external organization and system).
2. The enterprise business process (B) is completely new, with new IT applications to be built.
3. The enterprise business process (C) also represents an enhancement over the current situation, but with the two impacted teams being internal to the company.

Applications / Enterprise processes	Order Team	Distribution Team	Procurement Team	Finance Team	External Service Company
Current Enterprise Process	X	X		X	
Future Enterprise Process (A)	X	X		X	X
Current Enterprise Process (N/A)	X	X	X		
Future Enterprise Process (B)	X	X			
Current Enterprise Process	X	X	X	X	
Future Enterprise Process (C)	X		X	X	

Figure 7.31 Gaps in enterprise IT applications.

Data Entity	Future IT Applications			
	App #1	App #2	App #3	App #4
Data entity #1	C/U			
Data entity #2		C/U		
Data entity #3				C/U
Data entity #4			C/U	
Etc.				

Note: C = Create; U = Update.

Figure 7.32   Data creation and update by future IT applications.

7.4.3 Gaps in Enterprise IT Data Architecture

7.4.3.1 Transactional Applications

An example of a gap in this company's enterprise IT data architecture could be, as previously explained, that only one application should be allowed, going forward, to create and update a single set of data entities. This is shown in Figure 7.32.

7.4.3.2 Enterprise Business Intelligence/Analytics

As for IT data architecture gaps in terms of business intelligence/analytics, an example could be that some existing data marts have been allowed to be built with data feeds that are not part of the enterprise data warehouse (EDW), but that should no longer be the case going forward (Figure 7.33).

While the batch environment we describe above in terms of transactional and analytical enterprise data architecture should apply to an overwhelming majority of organizations, there is a new trend in the IT industry to provide a new technology platform for massive parallel and real-time analytical data processing, such as from SAP Corp. or IBM, that you may want to keep an eye on.

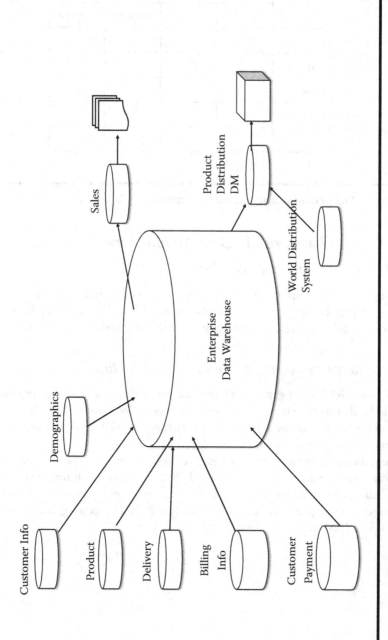

Figure 7.33   Future BI data architecture.

7.4.4 Gaps in Enterprise IT Infrastructure Architecture

It cannot be emphasized enough how significant of a difference your organization's IT infrastructure can make in terms of competitive advantage and traditional cost saving.

One of the more renowned examples demonstrating such a gain was Lenovo's purchase of IBM's PC and laptop business. As discussed in the previously mentioned *Wall Street Journal* article, "How Lenovo Pulled the Plug on IBM's Legacy," Lenovo had to overhaul the entire IBM PC Business Unit's out-of-date IT infrastructure before it could fully take advantage of the synergy that it had hoped would come along with the acquisition of the IBM PC Business Unit. Luckily, the benefits, as reported, far outweighed the pain of the challenging transition. In completing the migration to the new IT infrastructure, Lenovo has since been able to achieve a significant improvement in manufacturing, logistics, and ordering: up to 50% improvement in on-time deliveries, increased cost savings in terms of adding new shippers, as well as reduced costs of logistics and material overhead—everything a business can hope to expect from its IT.

Now, to return to our review of the different enterprise architecture layers, Figures 7.34 and 7.35 are two depictions of the gaps with respect to enterprise infrastructure architecture for both transactional and business intelligence.

Transactional Applications	Infrastructure		
	(1) Database	*(2) Servers*	*(3) Network Bandwidth*
Application #1	10 GB	5 servers 2.4 GHz 2 GB RAM	T1
Application #2	1 TB	15 servers 2.4 GHz quad-core 8 GB RAM	Fiber
Application #3	200 GB	6 servers 3 GHz dual-core 4 GB RAM	T3

Figure 7.34   Gaps in enterprise IT infrastructure architecture: Transactional.

BI Applications	Infrastructure		
	(1) Database	*(2) Servers*	*(3) Network Bandwidth*
Application #1	50 GB	10 servers 2.4 GHz dual-core 2 GB RAM	T3
Application #2	35 GB	10 servers 2.4 GHz dual-core 2 GB RAM	T1
Application #3	750 GB	12 servers 2.4 GHz quad-core 4 GB RAM	Fiber
Application #4	2 GB	1 server 2.4 GHz 1 GB RAM	T1
Application #5	5 GB	2 servers 2.4 GHz 2 GB RAM	T1

Figure 7.35   Gaps in enterprise IT infrastructure architecture: Business intelligence.

As a summary of all of our previous discussions regarding the gaps between the current situation and future needs, Figure 7.36 depicts the conceptual end result—to be filled with an organization's specific names of business processes and IT applications as well as databases and servers.

As previously mentioned, while Figure 7.36 is a conceptual architectural diagram, Figure 7.37 represents an architectural style declination of the previous diagram, using an SOA architectural style.

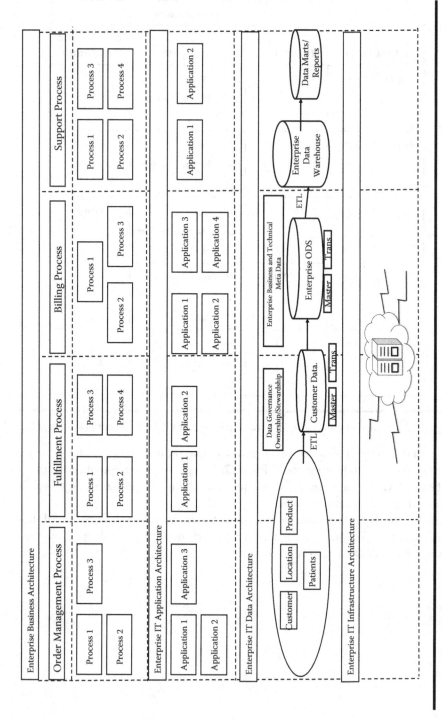

Figure 7.36 The organization's future enterprise architecture.

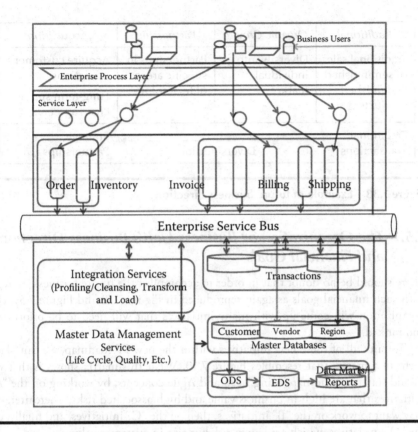

Figure 7.37   The organization's enterprise architecture with SOA.

7.5 Step 4: Identify the IT Roadmap

Once all of the business and IT gaps have been identified with the previous step, you will now have the foundation of the future IT roadmap.

As we wrap up our discussion on business strategy and the IT roadmap, let us sum it up by saying that you should have the following five artifacts by the end of this undertaking:

1. The organization or business unit's business direction and financial goals
2. The organization or business unit's overall enterprise architecture
3. Technical migration plan
4. Timeline
5. Budget

Now that we have seen the list, let us review these items, one by one, to make sure that we know what they are and how they fit with one another.

Traditional	Organic Growth	Partnership	Acquisition
Traditional sale of semifinished and finished products	Diversify into individual markets	Partnerships in specific areas of technology	Acquire customer's operations Long-term supply chain agreement
Traditional Transactions	Diversification ————————————→		Strategic Partnerships

Figure 7.38 Example of future business direction.

7.5.1 The Organization or Business Unit's Business Direction and Financial Goals

There should be no doubt that in order to accomplish the future business strategy with such financial goals as again reproduced in Figure 7.38 and Figure 7.39, the organization will come up with many initiatives that will need to be prioritized and ranked.

To rank all of these new initiatives within the new IT roadmap, we can place them in a matrix that resembles Figure 7.40. What this matrix shows is that we should start the roadmap, using Lean and Agile concepts, by working on the "A" initiatives that are high in business value and high associated risks. Thereafter, we may want to work on the "B" initiatives, then on the "C" initiatives, and finally, on the "D" initiatives, which are low in risk but also in customer value.

Business Goals Projections

Items	Base Year	Year 1	Year 2	Year 3
Annual revenue growth rate	20%	20%	25%	30%
Revenue	$30,000,000	$36,000,000	$45,000,000	$58,500,000
Cost of goods sold (as % of revenue)	20%	18%	16%	14%
Cost of goods sold	–$6,000,000	–$6,480,000	–$7,200,000	–$8,190,000
Sales & marketing expenses (as % of revenue)	15%	15%	10%	10%
General & administrative expenses (as % of revenue)	10%	10%	5%	5%
Depreciation expenses	–$300,000	–$300,000	–$300,000	–$300,000
Tax rate	35%	35%	35%	35%

Figure 7.39 Example of business goals.

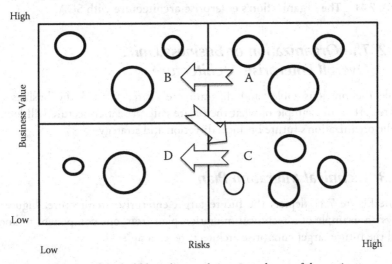

Note: The size of the bubble indicates the projected cost of the project.

Figure 7.40 New IT applications prioritization matrix.

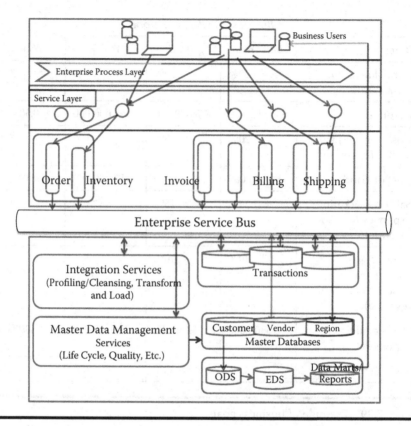

Figure 7.41 The organization's enterprise architecture with SOA.

7.5.2 The Organization or Business Unit's Overall Enterprise Architecture

While the previous tables and diagram are geared toward the business side, Figure 7.41 is an example of what the future enterprise architecture will look like for the organization's future business direction and strategy.

7.5.3 Technical Migration Plan

While Figure 7.41 depicts the future target enterprise architecture, Figure 7.42 shows an example of a technical migration plan from one component to another until the future target enterprise architecture is completed.

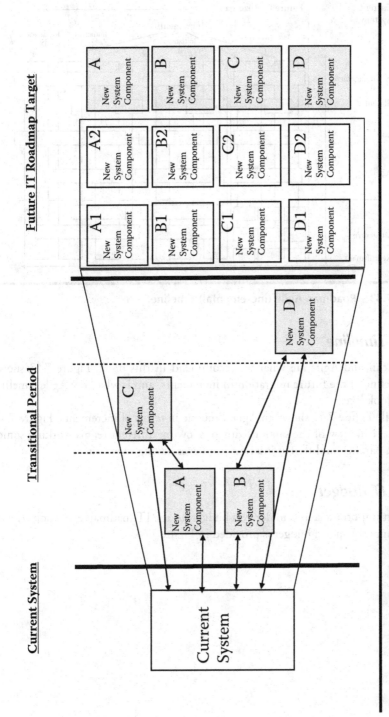

Figure 7.42 IT roadmap technical component transition.

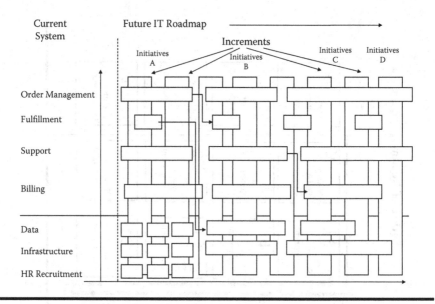

Figure 7.43 Roadmap Agile (incremental) timeline.

7.5.4 Timeline

Since Lean and Agile are what we recommend in this book, Figure 7.43 shows the timeline of the future migration in increments, and is what any Agile timeline should look like.

While Figure 7.43 shows an Agile timeline in terms of increments, Figure 7.44 shows a Lean view of the same roadmap, showing different teams working sometimes in parallel on different iniatives but never having to multitask.

7.5.5 IT Budget

The next important step is to derive a budget for the IT roadmap execution. A partial example of such a budget is provided in Figure 7.45.

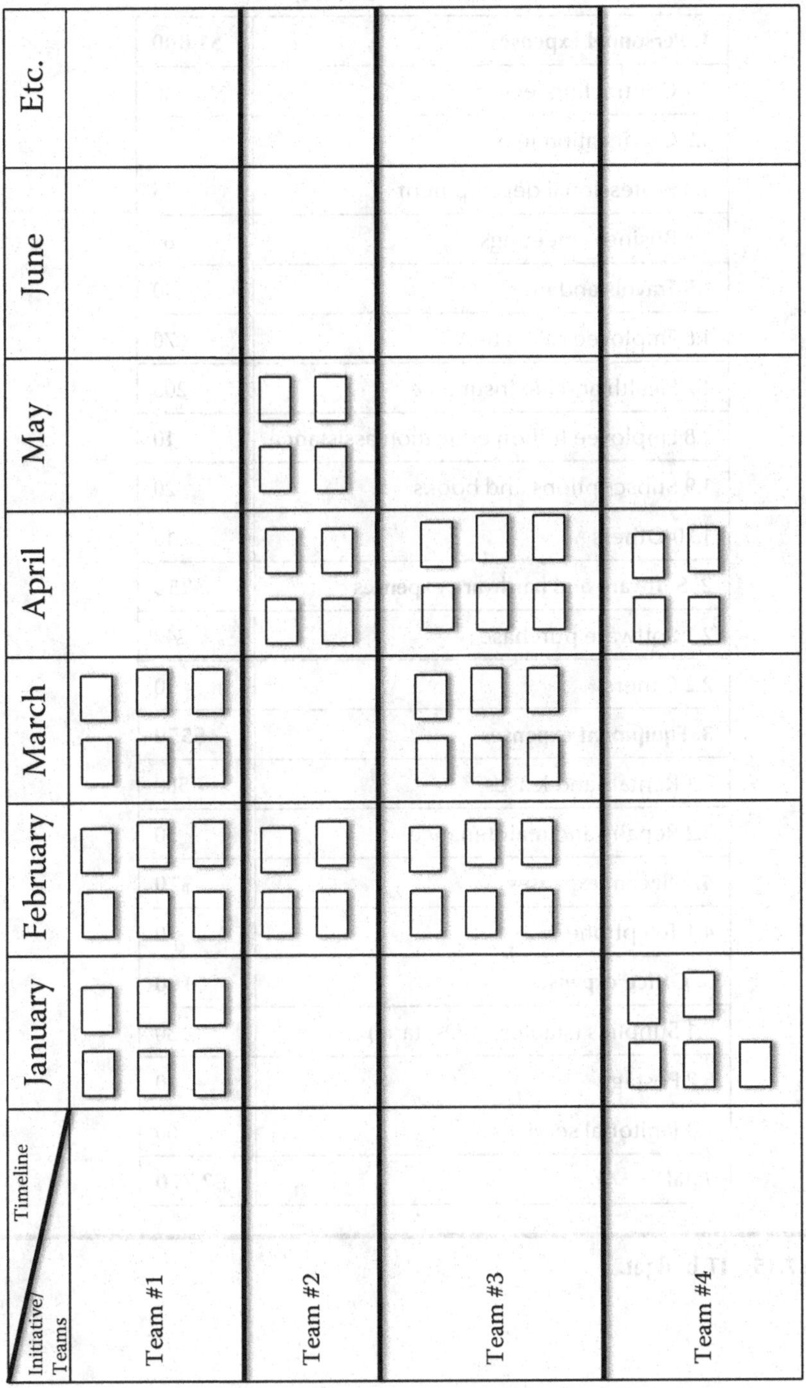

Timeline — Initiative/Teams	January	February	March	April	May	June	Etc.
Team #1	□□□ □□	□□□ □□□	□□□ □□□				
Team #2		□□ □□		□□ □□	□□ □□		
Team #3		□□□ □□□	□□□ □□□	□□□ □□□			
Team #4	□□ □□□			□□ □□			

Figure 7.44 A Lean view of the roadmap timeline: Teams without multitasking.

IT Budget ($ in thousands)

1. Personnel expenses	**$1,800**
1.1 Contracting fees	1,300
1.2 Certification fees	25
1.3 Professional development	15
1.4 Business meetings	60
1.5 Travels and meals	90
1.6 Employee relocations	70
1.7 Health and life insurance	200
1.8 Employee tuition education assistance	10
1.9 Subscriptions and books	20
1.10 Others	10
2. Software and hardware expenses	**$250**
2.1 Software purchase	240
2.2 Others	10
3. Equipment expenses	**$550**
3.1 Rentals and leases	500
3.2 Repairs and maintenance	50
4. Telecom expenses	**$70**
4.1 Telephone	70
5. Office expenses	**$100**
5.1 Supplies (staplers, CDs, tape)	30
5.2 Postage	10
5.3 Janitorial services	60
Total	**$2,770**

Figure 7.45   IT budget.

7.6 Takeaways

Although we have made the process of creating an IT roadmap as simple and straightforward as possible, this does not mean that the process is only applicable to small and midsize commercial companies and nonprofit associations. In fact, most of our experiences come directly from IT roadmaps created within multibillion-dollar companies. While the process we used works for a large organization, it is worth remembering that documenting a business strategy and creating an IT roadmap for a small- or medium-size organization often requires much less detail than would be needed for a larger organization.

To sum up the key points of the process that we discussed in this chapter:

- When working on the enterprise business architecture, we strongly suggest that you put emphasis on the customer-facing and supplier/partner-facing processes in order to bring the most value to your customers or constituents.
- When working on the enterprise IT application architecture, remember to assess both transactional applications (such as order entry or shipping and billing) and BI or analytical applications (such as product margin or regional sales).
- When working on the enterprise IT data architecture, make sure that you do not allow a data entity to be created or updated by more than one IT application. Likewise, set up a new layer of reference databases called master databases in order to reduce the likelihood that a multitude of data entities become a source of data inconsistency.
- When working on the enterprise IT infrastructure, remember that it is not simply a bunch of computer equipment, but something that can positively or negatively influence your organization's ability to serve your customers or constituents.

Regarding the gaps, start with the current enterprise business processes, which you will derive and then try to improve with your organization's new business direction. Next, lay the new enterprise business processes over these current business process to identify the gaps that need to be filled.

Once you have finished, carry out the same process with diagrams of the enterprise IT application architecture layer, then the enterprise IT data architecture layer, and finally, the enterprise IT infrastructure layer. As needed, repeat the process with the enterprise security architecture layer— if it is something of importance to your organization.

All in all, you should have the following artifacts to make sure that your IT roadmap is completed and aligned with the organization's new business strategy:

1. The organization or business unit's business direction and financial goals
2. The organization or business unit's overall enterprise architecture
3. Technical migration plan
4. Timeline
5. Budget

Chapter 8

From a Business Unit's IT Roadmap to an Enterprise IT Roadmap

---

8.1 Chapter Objective

This chapter walks you, the reader, through the process of creating an IT roadmap for the overall enterprise, starting from one created for only one strategic business unit (SBU).

8.2 The "What"

Rather than beginning with an enterprise IT roadmap, some organizations (especially the larger ones) start, more often than not, with a roadmap for only one of its strategic business units or departments.

As this first undertaking becomes more successful and generates momentum, the organization may turn its individual IT roadmap into an enterprise-wide undertaking, following a process similar to the one shown in Figure 8.1.

8.3 The "How"

Viewed from a different angle, the process an organization may follow when moving from a local roadmap to an enterprise-wide one also could resemble Figure 8.2.

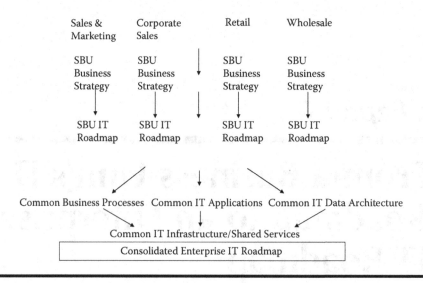

Figure 8.1 From a business unit's IT roadmap to an enterprise IT roadmap.

Examining Figure 8.2 more closely, we can see that as more local or SBU road-maps are being built at the same time, an effort should be made to turn similar business processes into a common set of enterprise business processes. The same logic should apply for turning similar IT applications into common enterprise IT applications and similar services or resources into common and shared services and resources.

8.4 Takeaways

Whether you like it or not, you may be asked to help formulate an IT roadmap for one strategic business unit (SBU) first.

If this is the case, then remember that when you are asked to leverage that foundation to build an IT roadmap for the entire organization, turn similar business processes, IT applications, databases, and infrastructure into common business processes, IT applications, databases, and shared infrastructure as well as shared services.

Approach for an Integrated IT Roadmap

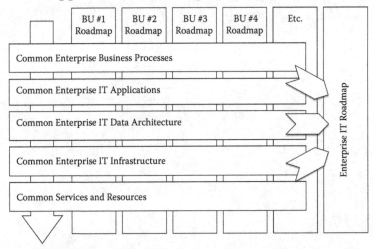

Figure 8.2   From a business unit's IT roadmap to an enterprise IT roadmap.

Chapter 9

IT and Mergers and Acquisitions (M&A) Activities

9.1 Chapter Objective

The objective of this chapter is to introduce the importance of taking IT into account early on in the M&A process, rather than letting it be an afterthought. In support of this, there will be an example of an IT due diligence questionnaire from which you can draw inspiration. Unlike most existing questionnaires, this one uses an enterprise architecture (EA) framework similar to the one we have reviewed in this book, in order to help gather data and assess the situation as well as evaluate if the merger would be desirable and, if so, under what conditions.

9.2 Mergers and Acquisitions Evaluation Process

Because IT is often considered an afterthought and not a strategic component of an organization's business strategy, numerous companies make the grave mistake of overlooking IT when they decide whether or not to merge with or acquire another organization.

Given that the purpose of this book is to highlight the strategic value that a well-aligned IT can bring to an organization, we recommend that the IT team be involved very early on in the M&A process. IT should even be part of the preliminary discussions as much as possible, as noted in the following evaluation process (which is largely focused on the technology side):

1. **Preliminary Discussions:** At this stage, senior management will begin receiving information about the other organization's financials. To the extent possible, the organization's finance, marketing, and business development executives should begin to form informal assessments, and IT executives should be asked to do the same.
2. **Candidate Evaluation:** By this time, a clear candidate has emerged for merger or acquisition, and the true evaluation process will begin.
3. **Due Diligence:** This stage provides everyone, including IT, with the opportunity to obtain all of the information needed to conduct due diligence. In particular, we recommend that IT use the different layers of the EA to perform this evaluation.
4. **Strategic Alignment and System Integration Opportunities:** The IT team should present any discoveries that may help to clarify potential synergies and integration opportunities between the two organizations. The IT team also should present all of the associated technology risks, costs, and potential trade-offs.
5. **Recommendation by IT Executive Management:** The IT team should formally provide its final recommendation to senior management, which may ultimately impact the cost of the M&A transaction.
6. **Board Review:** Next, the IT team should participate in a board review, answering any questions the board may have regarding its final recommendation.
7. **Final Decision:** The board will make the final decision as to whether or not the organization should proceed with the merger or acquisition.

9.3 IT Due Diligence Questionnaire

When IT conducts due diligence, in addition to other criteria, it should base its evaluation on the different layers of the EA. A questionnaire similar to the one found in Figure 9.1 would facilitate such an evaluation.

9.4 Takeaways

Too often, IT is considered only an afterthought during the M&A process. However, it is important to realize that knowing the other party's technology situation may have an impact not only on the price of the M&A valuation, but also how successful the system integration will be. Thus, we recommend that, within your own organization, you get IT involved early on in the M&A process and, if possible, use the different EA layers, as previously described in this book, as a reference guide during due diligence.

IT Due Diligence Questionnaire

1. Enterprise Business Architecture	Answer
1.1 Please state your business units' goals and metrics. How do you think you have achieved or are achieving them?	
1.2 Do you think your IT is clearly aligned with all of your business units' goals? Please list these goals, and provide data showing how IT has stated or proved that they can deliver on these goals?	
1.3 Do you have a clear understanding of who the business owners of all the IT applications are? Please provide a full list.	
1.4 How many enterprise processes do you have? How many are customer-facing processes? How many are supplier-facing processes?	
1.5 What kind of evaluation would you give to assess how you have been performing your customer-facing processes?	
1.6 What kind of evaluation would you give to assess how you have been performing your supplier-facing processes?	
1.7 Is there any duplication between different customer-facing enterprise processes?	
1.8 Is there any duplication between different supplier-facing enterprise processes?	
1.9 Is there any team who may be overloaded?	

Figure 9.1 IT due diligence questionnaire.

IT Due Diligence Questionnaire

2. Enterprise IT Application Architecture	Answer
2.1 How many transactional applications do you have?	
2.2 Is there any overlap between these transactional applications? Please provide a detailed list.	
2.3 Have you clearly identified what business units own which data entities?	
2.4 Have you performed an architectural evaluation of these applications? What was the result? Which ones should be decommissioned and which ones should be retired?	
2.5 Is there any duplication between different customer-facing or supplier-facing enterprise processes?	
2.6 How many interfaces have you identified between these applications? How many are real-time, and how many are batch interfaces? Please provide a complete list.	
2.7 What applications do you think would need to be renovated ASAP?	
2.8 What applications do you think would need to be retired? What is your plan for their replacement?	
2.9 What is your usage level of Lean and Agile in application software development?	

Figure 9.1 (continued) IT due diligence questionnaire.

IT Due Diligence Questionnaire

3. Enterprise IT Data Architecture	Answer
3.1 Are there any well-known inconsistencies between financial reports, such that the same data results are different? What is your plan to remedy this situation?	
3.2 What level of Master Data Management (MDM) do you have in place? Please provide details.	
3.3 Do you have performance-related issues with users trying to retrieve reports that take too long to come up?	
3.4 How many BI applications do you have? For whom?	
3.5 How many data sources do you have?	
3.6 Do you have an Operational Data Store (ODS)? For what reasons? What is the volume?	
3.7 Do you have an Enterprise Data Warehouse (EDW)? Why? What is the volume?	
3.8 Do you have a plan to improve your transactional and business intelligence (BI) IT data architecture?	
3.9 Do you have any data entity that is updated by more than one transactional application? Why?	

Figure 9.1 (continued) IT due diligence questionnaire.

IT Due Diligence Questionnaire

4. Enterprise IT Infrastructure Architecture	Answer
4.1 What is your current infrastructure in terms of equipment and volume? Please describe.	
4.2 How many servers do you have? What transactional or BI applications consume the majority of the servers? Why?	
4.3 Have you ever had any production outages?	
4.4 How often did you have these production outages? How long did it take you to fix them? Was there any impact in terms of loss of business?	
4.5 Have you ever identified the root causes of the production outages? What would be the long-term solution?	
4.6 Do you have a new roadmap for the IT infrastructure?	
4.7 What do you like the most about your current infrastructure? What do you worry the most about?	
4.8 What would be the most difficult obstacles to overcome in terms of trying to improve the infrastructure? Financial or technical?	

Figure 9.1 (continued) IT due diligence questionnaire.

Chapter 10

Change Management

10.1 Chapter Objective

The objective of this chapter is to introduce you to the need of setting up a plan that will help manage the changes that come with the creation and execution of a business strategy and IT roadmap. This will ultimately help you obtain buy-in from the troops and ease the transition.

10.2 Key Recommendations

Developing a business strategy and IT roadmap is something that can create both excitement and anxiety within an organization's ranks. After all, the resulting effort and change that come with it will impact everyone within the organization for a long time to come. As a seasoned executive, you would be right to contemplate how you would enact such change in a way that benefits both employees and the organization. Over the years, we have observed different cases wherein management considered such a transformation to be a discrete undertaking and, for this reason, avoided making an announcement, instead involving only a set of select senior employees they had chosen to inform of the change. Having ourselves been involved in similar experiences, we ultimately believe there is little justification for this attitude. Rather, we believe that management should make a formal announcement in order to build up momentum and excitement for this type of enterprise undertaking.

Naturally, top management must also take all of the necessary precautions to ease the concerns that may arise along with the excitement, managing expectations to ensure that employees are not disappointed if the effort unintentionally falls through after the first few weeks of excitement. The best thing for a CEO to do is formally inform all employees of the undertaking, explaining the reasons for it by elaborating on whether it is for the organization's survival or growth—or both.

With regards to timing, we cannot emphasize enough that the sooner a clear communication plan is devised and put into action, the better the reaction and feedback will be as management informs impacted employees of changes. So, do not forget about communication planning at the beginning of your future business strategy and IT roadmap formulation initiative.

Having made the above recommendation, it will be important for management to next mobilize the troops. To this end, we recommend that working groups be organized along the current functional structure (such as marketing, operations, sales, finance, etc.), even if, as a result of the undertaking, the organization ends up merging or removing different functions or teams. Starting with the current structure will enable the organization to manage its employees' transition into the future, without creating radically major disruption or high levels of anxiety.

On top of this, we recommend that these working groups also be organized to correspond to the four (or five) layers of the enterprise architecture: one should focus on the enterprise business direction and architecture; another should work on the enterprise IT application layer; another should investigate issues related to the enterprise IT data architecture; and the last should delve further into the enterprise IT infrastructure architecture.

The reason why we recommend that working groups be divided in this manner is to ensure that work can be carried out in parallel, thereby facilitating progress while also saving time. That being said, with different groups functioning in parallel, it also would be wise to organize a coordination group, in order to ensure the effective coordination and accurate synthesis of results from the different working groups.

Prior to the working groups' work on the above, we recommend that management take a short pause to encourage employees not to feel concerned about job impact and attempt to influence the organization's future direction. Every effort should be made to clarify that, should certain positions be removed, the impacted employees will be offered other positions or else, in the worst case scenario, severance packages that would take care of them and their families during their transitions to other companies.

The above being said, should the organization decide to pursue a complete restructuring, it would be key to obtain employees' buy-in, thereby encouraging creative and innovative thinking with regards to the organization's future structure, products, and services. Thus, management must make it clear ahead of time, before employees begin to express fears regarding job impact and attempt to influence the organization's future direction, that it is both in the organization's and the employees' best interest that no one hold back in their efforts to help the organization become more agile and innovative.

To this effect, before the executive team and working groups decide how to reorganize the organization's business processes and team structure, top management—particularly the CEO—should invite everyone to propose ideas for creating the most innovative and Lean (and, therefore, Agile) organization possible without fearing for their jobs.

Once the future team structure is decided, along with all of the supporting responsibilities, top management, such as the CEO (or CIO, if the reorganization only impacts IT), should formally let everyone know of the decision and explain why it will be best for the organization's new business strategy or social mission.

With regards to timing, we cannot emphasize enough that the sooner a clear communication plan is devised and put into action, the better the reaction and feedback will be as management informs impacted employees of changes. So, do not forget about communication planning at the beginning of your future business and IT roadmap formulation initiative.

For every enterprise undertaking that is transformative by nature, such as the one we describe in this book, it will be key for the organization to take precautions as it manages the transition from its current structure and operations into the future. If you would like to read more about the art of business strategy execution and change management, the books *Execution: The Discipline of Getting Things Done* by Larry Bossidy and Ram Charan and *Business-Driven IT-Wide Agile and Lean Implementation: An Action Guide for Business and IT Leaders* by Andrew Pham and David Pham are an excellent sources of ideas and reflection.[1,2]

Per our own experience, we strongly recommend that coaches and trainers be made available to help the team leaders manage each new team's adjustment toward the future business processes, IT applications, and procedures, with respect to the future business direction of the organization.

10.3 Takeaways

An undertaking such as creating an IT roadmap will no doubt bring quite a bit of stress and concern to the employees within an organization. You should plan and manage the impact of such an endeavor early on and throughout the process. The main message to your employees should be based on transparency, truth, and excitement.

Why transparency? We believe transparency helps reduce (if not eliminate) rumors, which can easily destroy employees' spirits and make such an undertaking very difficult to accomplish.

Why truth? While it may sound cliché, we firmly believe that being truthful is key to winning people's minds and hearts.

Why excitement? We believe that there should be a reason to send a message of enthusiasm to the organization, especially when identifying the organization's new business strategy and creating an IT roadmap to help make the organization grow.

Reference

1. Bossidy, L., and R. Charan. 2002. *Execution: The discipline of getting things done.* New York: Crown Business.
2. Pham, A., and D. Pham. 2012. *Business-driven IT-wide Agile (Scrum) and Lean (Kanban) implementation: An action guide for business and IT leaders.* New York: Productivity Press.

FROM IT ROADMAP FORMULATION TO EXECUTION

V

It may sound cliché to say that strategy is execution, as the late management guru Peter Drucker used to say—but it is true. Unless you can execute your business strategy or IT roadmap, it will only be a few ideas on paper—no more, no less.

Chapter 11

Strategy Is Execution

Having a business strategy is undoubtedly a good first step, but truly, anyone can come up with a business strategy or IT roadmap so long as he or she does not have to execute it. This is why we are going to offer you, in the following pages, several suggestions on how to get organized so that you can efficiently execute your strategy or roadmap.

11.1 Chapter Objective

This chapter introduces you to IT roadmap execution, describing how to get organized as well as how and what to review for the execution of your IT roadmap. Our aim is to ensure that this produces the results you are looking for.

11.2 Getting Organized for Execution

Depending on your organization's situation, size, and culture, you are not going to get organized the same way when seeing through your organization's IT roadmap execution. That being said, based on what we have gone through, we can divide your execution organization into two units: (1) the Business and IT Governance Board and (2) the Business Unit IT Steering Committee.

11.2.1 Business and IT Governance Board

The Business and IT Governance Board is the committee at the enterprise level that, under the CEO's direction, is responsible for reviewing and approving the IT roadmap with regards to the organization's business strategy.

Once the IT roadmap has been approved, the board reviews and approves all business technology requests that may impact the underlying enterprise architecture and, therefore, the organization's business strategy.

While the CEO must preside over this board, the CIO (Chief Information Officer) or CTO (Chief Technology Officer) should serve as the Secretary of this board, with the Chief Architect as his deputy. The Chief Architect should be in charge of organizing the board review meetings and the enterprise architecture (EA) review, especially when it comes to overseeing requests for new business technology investment approval.

This board should meet at least once every three months or as frequently as needs arise that require its attention.

11.2.2 Business Unit IT Steering Committee

While the Board and the IT Steering Committee may be the same in small organizations, they should be two distinctive groups in larger organizations.

In large organizations, this Business Unit IT Steering Committee is, at the business unit level, responsible for reviewing and approving business technology requests that do not go against the overall organization's business strategy and that do not have an impact on the overall enterprise architecture.

The CIO should serve as the Co-President of the Committee, alongside the Vice President or Senior Vice President in charge of the business unit. This committee should meet at least once a month or as often as needed to review new business technology requests.

11.3 What to Review?

11.3.1 Business Goals Review

Assuming that an organization has originally set up the goals featured in Figure 11.1 to Figure 11.4, a business goals review will be an opportunity to evaluate how much the IT roadmap execution has allowed the organization to reach its goals.

As Figure 11.1 demonstrates, the company is aiming to increase its revenue and decrease its sales and marketing expenses over the next three years. Concurrently, management projects that the company's cost of goods sold will rise, which may negatively impact operating profits during this term, as shown in the income statement in Figure 11.2.

Management further understands that they will need to increase property, plant, and equipment (PP&E) vital to business operations over the next three years. However, the company will continue to focus on enhancing cash flow during this timeframe. These company goals are exhibited in the cash flow statement and balance sheet shown in Figure 11.3 and Figure 11.4.

Business Goals Projections

Items	Base Year	Year 1	Year 2	Year 3
Annual revenue growth rate	5%	5%	10%	10%
Revenue	$7,000,000	$7,350,000	$8,085,000	$8,893,500
Costs of goods sold (as % of revenue)	35%	40%	45%	50%
Costs of goods sold	$2,450,000	$2,940,000	$3,638,250	$4,446,750
Sales & marketing expenses (as % of revenue)	30%	28%	27%	24%
General & administrative expenses (as % of revenue)	6%	6%	6%	6%
Depreciation	–$10,000	–$10,000	–$12,500	–$15,000
Tax rate	35%	35%	35%	35%

Figure 11.1   Example of business goals.

Pro Forma Income Statement

	Base Year	Year 1	Year 2	Year 3
Revenue	**$7,000,000**	**$7,350,000**	**$8,085,000**	**$8,893,500**
Raw materials	–420,000	–441,000	–485,100	–533,610
Direct labor costs	–2,030,000	–2,499,000	–3,153,150	–3,913,140
Cost of goods sold	**–$2,450,000**	**–$2,940,000**	**–$3,638,250**	**–$4,446,750**
Gross profit	**$4,550,000**	**$4,410,000**	**$4,446,750**	**$4,446,750**
Sales & marketing expenses	–2,100,000	–2,058,000	–2,182,950	–2,134,440
General & administrative expenses	–420,000	–441,000	–485,100	–533,610
Earnings before interest, taxes, depreciation & amortization	**$2,030,000**	**$1,911,000**	**$1,778,700**	**$1,778,700**
Depreciation expenses	–10,000	–10,000	–12,500	–15,000
Operating profit	**$2,020,000**	**$1,901,000**	**$1,766,200**	**$1,763,700**
Interest expense (Net)	–102,000	–73,950	–31,875	–10,838
Pretax income	**$1,918,000**	**$1,827,050**	**$1,734,325**	**$1,752,863**
Income taxes	–671,300	–639,468	–607,014	–613,502
Net income	**$1,246,700**	**$1,187,583**	**$1,127,311**	**$1,139,361**

Figure 11.2   Pro forma income statement.

Pro Forma Cash Flow Statement

	Base Year	Year 1	Year 2	Year 3
Net income		**$1,187,583**	**$1,127,311**	**$1,139,361**
Depreciation		10,000	12,500	15,000
Changes in working capital				
Accounts receivable		517,808	−120,822	−132,904
Inventory		−124,274	−179,421	−207,330
Accounts payable		17,548	49,537	33,226
Cash from operating activities		**$1,608,665**	**$889,106**	**$847,352**
Capital expenditures		−25,000	−30,000	−35,000
Other investment		0	0	0
Cash from investing activities		**−$25,000**	**−$30,000**	**−$35,000**
Net borrowing		−825,000	−412,500	−206,250
Dividends		0	0	0
Capital contributions		0	0	0
Cash from financing activities		**−$825,000**	**−$412,500**	**−$206,250**
Change in cash		**$758,665**	**$446,606**	**$606,102**

Figure 11.3   Pro forma cash flow statement.

Pro Forma Balance Sheet

	Base Year	Year 1	Year 2	Year 3
Assets				
Cash and cash equivalents	$5,488,892	$6,247,556	$6,694,162	$7,300,264
Accounts receivable	1,726,027	1,208,219	1,329,041	1,461,945
Inventories	673,151	797,425	976,845	1,184,176
Total current assets	**$7,888,070**	**$8,253,200**	**$9,000,049**	**$9,946,385**
Property, plant, and equipment	210,000	225,000	242,500	262,500
Goodwill	60,000	60,000	60,000	60,000
Total assets	**$8,158,070**	**$8,538,200**	**$9,302,549**	**$10,268,885**
Liabilities				
Accounts payable	$411,370	$428,918	$478,455	$511,681
Debt	1,500,000	675,000	262,500	56,250
Total liabilities	**$1,911,370**	**$1,103,918**	**$740,955**	**$567,931**
Stockholders' equity				
Starting stockholders' equity	$5,000,000	$6,246,700	$7,434,283	$8,561,594
Net income	1,246,700	1,187,583	1,127,311	1,139,361
Dividends	0	0	0	0
Capital contributions	0	0	0	0
Stockholders' equity	**$6,246,700**	**$7,434,283**	**$8,561,594**	**$9,700,954**
Total liabilities & equity	**$8,158,070**	**$8,538,200**	**$9,302,549**	**$10,268,885**

Figure 11.4   Pro forma balance sheet.

As progress on the IT roadmap is made, it also would be useful for both the business and IT executives to regularly review various charts, as seen in Figure 11. 5 to Figure 11.10, so that they may have a clearer picture of the contribution that the IT roadmap execution is making to the organization's future business strategy.

By looking at Figure 11.5, even though in this example the chart only provides a partial view into the annual revenue for Year 1, it does give us an idea regarding how often the actual business revenue has been less than planned. So, one of the questions that executives can ask is whether the IT investment has been worthwhile and how much IT has been able to contribute to the organization's bottom line.

Now, by looking at Figure 11.6, the organization seems, in this case, to have been able to make a steady increase in revenue, year to year.

Figure 11.7, however, indicates that the organization's profit margin seems to have declined more than expected. This, in return, leads us to wonder whether the organization has some issue with its enterprise cost structure. If this is confirmed, there may be an opportunity for business and IT executives to see if they can trim down the organization's enterprise cost or reorient the IT roadmap's direction toward realizing some more cost reduction.

Further supporting the decreasing pattern of the profit margin, Figure 11.8 confirms that the organization's earnings per share has also declined more than expected.

Despite the rather bad news uncovered from reviewing the previous two charts, a rather surprising trend is revealed by Figure 11.9, which shows a more than expected increase in the organization's cash flow.

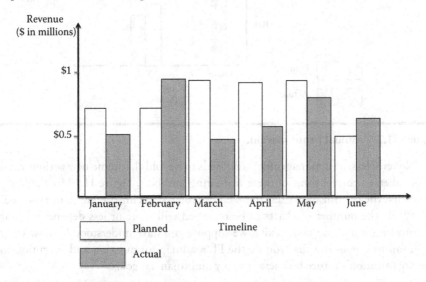

Figure 11.5   Business goals: Planned versus actual.

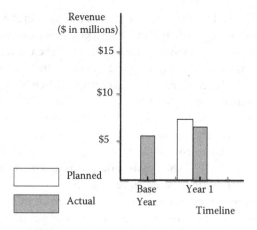

Figure 11.6   Annual revenue.

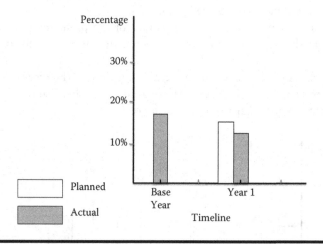

Figure 11.7   Annual profit margin.

Nonetheless, as if management still needs to be told that some new actions need to be taken to correct some of these worsening numbers, Figure 11.10 further confirms that the organization's return on equity too has declined more than expected.

While the number of charts to be reviewed will more or less depend on your organization's size and complexity, we suppose you have understood by now what we mean in suggesting that you tie the IT roadmap formulation and execution to the organization's future business strategy and financial goals.

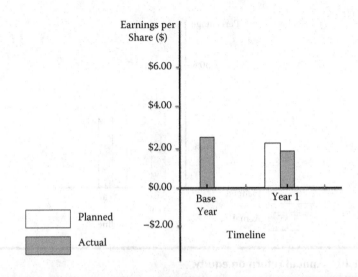

Figure 11.8 Annual earnings per share.

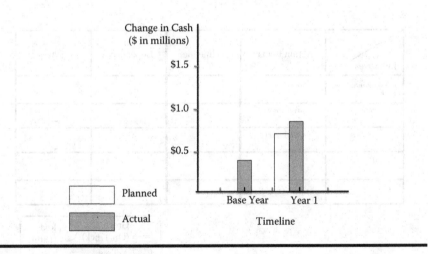

Figure 11.9 Annual cash flow.

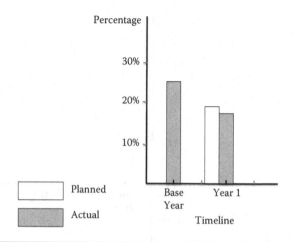

Figure 11.10 Annual return on equity.

11.3.2 IT Roadmap Execution Progress Review

If the previous review was to see how the IT roadmap was able to contribute to the organization's business strategy, Figure 11.11 is an example of how to keep an eye on the progress of the execution of the IT roadmap action items themselves in terms of their actual realization.

Initiatives	Action Items	Timeline	Dependency	Status
1. Order Management Track	Action Item #1			△
2. Fulfillment Track	Action Item #1			▢
3. Support Track	Action Item #1			◯
4. Billing Track				
Etc.				

△ Green (On Track)　◯ Red (Late)　▢ Yellow (Some Concern)

Figure 11.11 IT roadmap status by tracks.

11.3.3 IT Budget Review

While examining the progress of the IT roadmap execution, particular attention should be paid to the evolution of the budget in order to determine if the organization will need more funding to keep the execution on track and make it a more complete success (Figure 11.12).

11.4 Revision to the IT Roadmap

By regularly reviewing the situation of the business direction and the new financial goals, the organization will be able to make needed changes by either lowering the financial goals or by adjusting some of the IT roadmap initiatives without ever having to depart radically from its original intent. This said, on occasion, an organization will need to completely revise the direction of its business strategy and IT roadmap, as may especially happen in the event of a merger or acquisition.

11.5 Takeaways

In addition to reviewing the IT roadmap's budget and action items' progress during the IT roadmap execution period, make sure that your organization also reviews the situation of the business and financial goals during this timeframe.

Likewise, depending on your organization's context and situation, you should also feel free to adapt the organization of the IT roadmap execution review as well as how often these review meetings take place.

Last but not least, organizations should not have to depart radically from their business strategy or IT roadmap direction, but exceptions may occur, especially due to mergers and acquisitions.

IT Budget ($ in thousands)

	Planned	Actual
1. Personnel Expenses	**$1,220**	**$1,174**
1.1 Contracting Fees	1,000	1,000
1.2 Certification Fees	5	10
1.3 Professional Development	10	10
1.4 Business Meetings	10	7
1.5 Travels and Meals	50	10
1.6 Employee Relocations	20	15
1.7 Health and Life Insurance	100	100
1.8 Employee Tuition Education Assistance	5	5
1.9 Subscriptions and Books	10	7
1.10 Others	10	10
2. Software and Hardware Expenses	**$240**	**$220**
2.1 Software Purchase	220	200
2.2 Others	20	20
3. Equipment Expenses	**$500**	**$420**
3.1 Rentals and Leases	480	400
3.2 Repairs and Maintenance	20	20
4. Telecom Expenses	**$40**	**$30**
4.1 Telephone	40	30
5. Office Expenses	**$80**	**$75**
5.1 Supplies [Staplers, CD's, Tape]	20	20
5.2 Postage	10	5
5.3 Janitorial Services	50	50
Total	**$2,080**	**$1,919**

Figure 11.12   IT budget variance.

Chapter 12

Parting Thoughts

Congratulations on reaching the end of our book. Rather than letting you move ahead alone, here are some simple thoughts for reflection we would like to offer, in order to keep you company while you are on your way to a successful execution of your business strategy and IT roadmap.

- **Start anywhere, but at least start:** Nothing will ever be perfect in a business environment. It is just a fact of life.
- **Do not blame the business executives:** They are likely as eager as you are to attempt this endeavor.
- **Do not complain or whine; do not be part of the problem but part of the solution:** View everything as an opportunity to learn and to achieve something meaningful. This is not only true at work, but also in life.
- **Refine and learn from the first cut of your roadmap:** You may not be perfect when you first start, but after doing this for a short while, you will start to observe where you could eventually improve.
- **Find joy in creating something of value:** You will feel happy going home knowing that you are doing something valuable for the organization and for yourself.

Last but not least, remember that your organization's survival or growth may depend on this undertaking—so do your best before it is too late.

This is what has kept us hoping and going, and we hope it will keep you going as well.

Good luck to you!

CASE STUDIES

VI

To further illustrate the process of business strategy and IT roadmap formulation and execution, we have included two case studies. The subject of the first case study is a commercial company, All About HatWare, while the subject of the second case study is a nonprofit association, US Against Illiteracy.

Chapter 13

Case Study 1: Commercial Case Study: All About HatWare

For illustrative purposes, imagine that All About HatWare is a family-owned, hat manufacturing company that sells semifinished hats to a number of different companies. These companies then finish the hats and sell them under their own brand name.

In order to facilitate our review of this case study, we will be using the same diagram that we used in Chapter 7 (reproduced in Figure 13.1) to guide us through the process of creating All About HatWare's IT roadmap.

Discussing All About HatWare, we will, in following the contents of the book, cover the following aspects of its business:

13.1:   Current Enterprise Business Architecture
13.2:   Current Enterprise IT Application Architecture
13.3:   Current Enterprise IT Data Architecture
13.4:   Current Enterprise IT Infrastructure Architecture
13.5:   Future Business Strategy and Its New Enterprise Business Architecture
13.6:   Future Enterprise IT Application Architecture
13.7:   Future Enterprise IT Data Architecture
13.8:   Future Enterprise IT Infrastructure Architecture
13.9:   Gaps in Enterprise Business Processes
13.10: Gaps in Enterprise IT Application Architecture

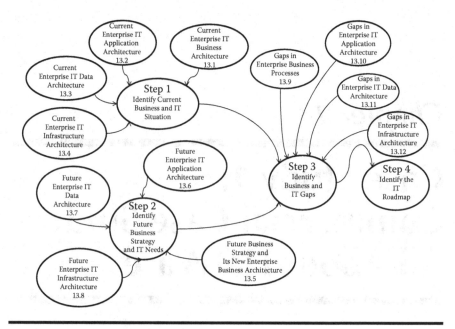

Figure 13.1   Detailed IT roadmap formulation process.

13.1 Current Enterprise Business Architecture

There are three aspects of All About HatWare's current enterprise business architecture that we should review: business goals, business processes, and team structure.

13.1.1 Business Goals

Like many family-owned companies, All About HatWare's business goals and direction had never been formally defined.

Until recently, the various family members and business leaders who had come to work at the company since it was first founded by the current president's father had all had different personal perspectives as to what the company's strategy was.

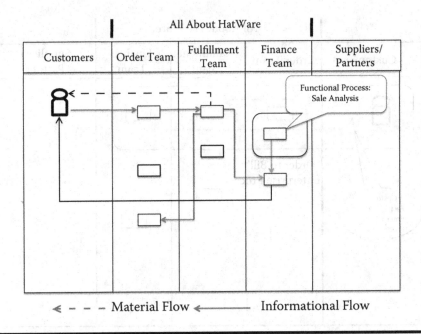

Figure 13.2 All About HatWare's functional processes.

13.1.2 Business Processes

As with many other family-owned enterprises, some simple enterprise and functional processes alone comprised the majority of All About HatWare's business processes. This is to say that different teams performed these different processes in order to accept orders, bill customers, and analyze sales (Figure 13.2), all in a rather fragmented way, without any regard for the organization's overall effectiveness.

Analyzing Figure 13.2, it is apparent that All About HatWare's main enterprise business process was the one used to take customers' orders.

This "order to bill" process is further broken down in Figure 13.3 and Figure 13.4. The chart in Figure 13.4 details some more intricacies, as needed, that are behind what initially appears to be a simple process.

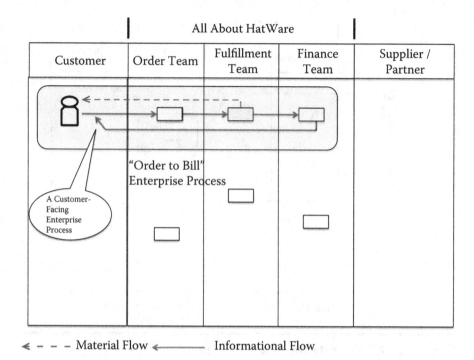

Material Flow ←   Informational Flow

Figure 13.3 **"Order to bill": An enterprise process within All About HatWare.**

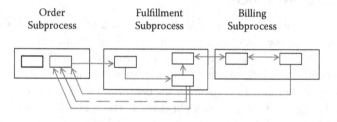

Figure 13.4 **Different components of the "order to bill" enterprise process.**

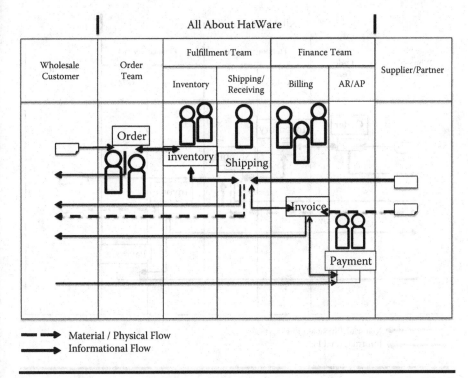

Figure 13.5 All About HatWare's current team structure.

13.1.3 Team Structure

At All About HatWare, the "order to bill" enterprise process leveraged a team structure that was organized around classic functions, such as order taking, shipping and delivery, and billing, as depicted in Figure 13.5.

Besides this, All About HatWare was itself a centralized organization where everyone was housed in one building.

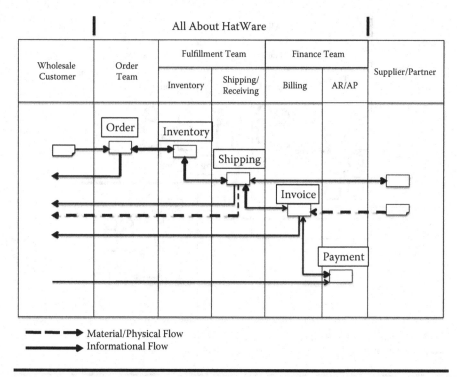

Figure 13.6 **All About HatWare's current enterprise IT application architecture.**

13.2 Current Enterprise IT Application Architecture

Now that we have gone through a brief review of the current enterprise business architecture, let us next look at All About HatWare's current enterprise IT application architecture.

As might be expected of a family business, their current enterprise IT application architecture was also characterized by some simple in-house software applications, which were all that All About HatWare used in support of its current business processes, as can be seen in Figure 13.6.

After all, All About HatWare's IT was first formed when the company was still very small. As a result, most of the in-house applications also started out small and grew into what they are today, though not without shortcomings.

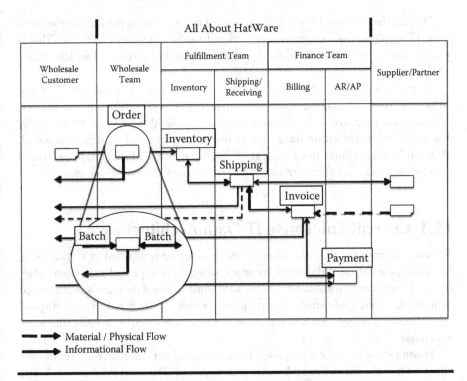

Material / Physical Flow
Informational Flow

Figure 13.7   Some of All About HatWare's batch application interfaces.

Processes	IT Applications				
	Order	Inventory	Shipping	Billing	AR/AP
Order to procure	X	X			
Order to bill	X			X	
Inventory to stock		X	X		
Order to cash	X	X			X

Figure 13.8   All About HatWare's IT applications by business processes.

Given the fact that most of All About HatWare's processes were rather simple, most (if not all) of the interfaces between its supporting software applications also were simple batch interfaces (Figure 13.7). Consequently, customer orders required at least 48 hours before they could be confirmed, if not longer.

In an effort to understand which IT applications supported which processes, we can summarize these findings in the table shown in Figure 13.8.

Despite the fact that IT was not considered the most strategic asset of the company, IT applications were considered critical to the company's business. This is why we should next analyze which applications should remain and which should be retired.

By performing an architectural assessment of the current transactional applications, as shown in Figure 13.9, we can see that several of the current applications may have needed to be decommissioned. Applications #3 and #5 especially deserved further renovation since their ratings were generally low across the board. Meanwhile, other applications, such as #1 and #2, should be functionally enhanced because their functional business alignments had considerably low ratings of 1.

13.3 Current Enterprise IT Data Architecture

The current enterprise IT transactional data architecture is depicted in Figure 13.10. Reviewing the different databases by application, there appeared to be some overlaps and consequent inconsistencies because some of the data were being updated by more than one application. This frequently resulted in different reports displaying differing numbers, even when these reports were calculated using the same data fields.

Having examined the enterprise IT transactional data architecture, let us now take a look at the enterprise IT business intelligence (BI) data architecture to better understand how things were going.

By studying Figure 13.11, we can see why data reporting could appear to be inconsistent. Because some of the results were calculated from rogue data feeds that had not been validated, the numbers could risk not matching up.

Further evaluating these enterprise IT BI/analytics applications (as visualized in Figure 13.12), it appeared that at least three applications should either be retired or else renovated as they possessed average scores equal to or less than 2. These included applications #2, #3, and #5.

13.4 Current Enterprise IT Infrastructure Architecture

Not unlike other family businesses, All About HatWare appeared to maintain a rather basic infrastructure, with several servers running and being hosted within the four walls of the company itself.

Now that we have seen a snapshot of the current business and IT situation, let us next consider their future business strategy before we can finally show how All About HatWare created its IT roadmap to make its future business strategy happen.

Applications	Score Business Alignment	Maintainability	Architecture	Modularity	Minimum: 1 Maximum: 5 Scalability	Average Score
1. Order	1	4	5	4	4	3.6
2. Inventory	1	5	5	5	4	4.0
3. Shipping	2	2	2	2	2	2.0
4. Billing	2	3	3	4	5	3.4
5. AR/AP	2	2	1	3	2	2.0

Figure 13.9   All About HatWare's current IT transactional application architectural assessment.

	Current IT Applications				
Data	Order	Inventory	Shipping	Billing	AR/AP
Customer	C/R/U/D	U/R	U/R	U/R	
Order	C/U		U/R	U/R	
Product		C/U	R/U		

Note: C = Create; U = Update; D = Delete; R = Read.

Figure 13.10   IT data architecture by current transactional applications.

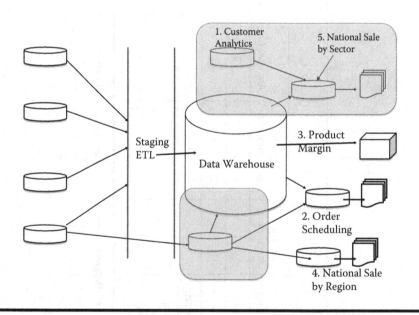

Figure 13.11   All About HatWare's current IT BI data architecture.

Applications	Score				Minimum: 1 Maximum: 5		
	Business Alignment	Maintainability	Architecture	Modularity	Scalability		Average Score
1. Customer analytics	2	5	3	1	4		3.0
2. Order scheduling	2	2	2	2	2		2.0
3. Product margin	2	2	2	2	2		2.0
4. National sale by region	2	5	4	3	3		3.4
5. National sale by sector	2	1	2	3	2		2.0

Figure 13.12   All About HatWare's current IT BI application architectural assessment.

13.5 Future Business Strategy and Its New Enterprise Business Architecture

13.5.1 Competitive Analysis

Up until now, the narrative behind All About HatWare had not been very notable. One day, however, a family reunion changed all of this. Given that the company's business revenue had flattened (as seen in Figure 13.13), the family came together and decided to use the framework described in our strategy section to formulate a new business strategy and direction in favor of more expansive growth.

Among other things, they wished to (1) transform the company from a wholesale company to a company that also would sell directly to individual customers and (2) leverage mobile and social network technologies whenever possible.

Using the competitive analysis techniques from Chapters 1 and 2, the family conducted an analysis that helped them to understand in which direction they should move in the future.

After closely analyzing All About HatWare's current strategy, the family found that it was internally consistent: The company's value chain activities were well-aligned to meet the needs of their various brand-name clients and provide them with semifinished hats. All About HatWare sold these hats at a relatively high price due to a strong willingness-to-pay among their customer base, given the high quality of the materials utilized and the recognized efficiency of All About HatWare's services.

That being said, however, the family also found that All About HatWare's current strategy was not externally consistent. In recent years, the company's brand-name clients had been consolidating due to a number of mergers, effectively creating larger apparel brands that were then able to take advantage of their scale to demand lower prices for All About HatWare's semifinished hats. Thus, with respect to Porter's Five Forces, the bargaining power of customers had been significantly increasing.

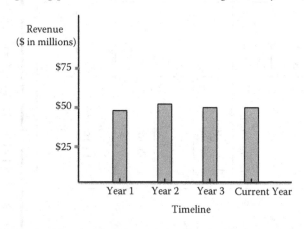

Figure 13.13   All About HatWare historical revenue.

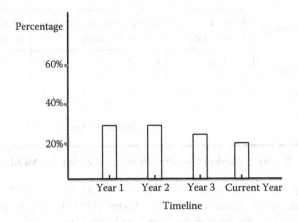

Figure 13.14 All About HatWare historical profit margin.

Simultaneously, these brand-name clients were demanding that All About HatWare continue increasing the quality of the materials used. However, a limited number of suppliers could offer such quality material. Thus, with respect to Porter's Five Forces, the bargaining power of these suppliers also was becoming quite excessive, driving up the overall costs of manufacturing hats. As a result, All About HatWare's profit margins had started to erode over time, as can be seen in Figure 13.14.

Meanwhile, the threat of new entrants was never-ending. Little capital was required to begin such a wholesale business, and All About HatWare was at risk of losing market share to new entrants by at least 5% to 10% by the next year. Substitutes also were continuous threats; in particular, the fashionable trend this year was to wear jackets and pea coats that included hoods, making hats unnecessary. Such a trend could be disastrous for All About HatWare's business because their apparel brand clients would easily be able to foresee this trend and gain additional bargaining power. Many clients, after all, also sold such hooded jackets and pea coats.

With regards to existing competitors, the fickle fashion tastes of the public lent to fierce rivalries. In addition, All About HatWare feared that their competitors had found ways to improve their own products and cost structure, providing a competitive advantage over All About HatWare. After conducting a relative cost analysis, All About HatWare found that the costs of production had indeed become cheaper for their competitors as a result of IT enhancements. As a result, the company found they would need to build new, more integrated software applications that could interact in real time with suppliers' and partners' technology applications.

The retail prices of hats in the United States were rising on average, but because All About HatWare had always sold its hats prior to them reaching end users (the individuals purchasing the hats), the company had never been able to establish their own brand and take part in this price hike.

		Current	Modified	New
Market	Current	Market Penetration	Partial Product/Service Diversification	Product Development
	New	Market Development	Partial Market Diversification	Diversification

Current   Modified   New

Product/Service

Figure 13.15 Product–Market Growth Directions Matrix for All About HatWare.

In developing the Strategy Blade for their business, it became increasingly apparent to the family members that All About HatWare was no longer setting itself apart and that competitors had exploited this lapse to move much further ahead. However, this issue could be overcome if All About HatWare began to focus on the individual market. Thus, the family decided that All About HatWare should begin to diversify from its wholesale business and find a way to also reach end users, selling these individuals finished hats branded under the company's own label. Because the company possessed existing relationships that could facilitate such distribution to noncompeting retailers, this transition would be feasible to execute.

All About HatWare next utilized the Product–Market Growth Directions Matrix to determine its business strategy. Assessing their present resources and large capacity for growth, the family decided to initially target an overall business mix of 50% sales from the individual market and 50% sales from the wholesale market. Thus, their strategy encompassed partial market diversification, selling their slightly modified hats to this new market of individuals (Figure 13.15).

13.5.2 All About HatWare's New Business Strategy

13.5.2.1 Future Goals and Direction

As a summary of the above analysis, the CEO spent time during his next meeting reminding everyone of what the company's new business direction would encompass:

- Transition from a semifinished product company to a finished product company.
- Sell not only to wholesale customers, but also to individual customers.
- Leverage new mobile and social networks for marketing purposes.
- Save enterprise costs by working more closely with suppliers and partners while also leveraging technologies to the maximum.
- Review and enhance IT applications to better meet new business needs.
- Enhance customer value creation by more significantly leveraging enterprise business processes.

Business Goals Projections

Items	Base Year	Year 1	Year 2	Year 3
Annual revenue growth rate	8%	10%	10%	10%
Revenue	$50,000,000	$55,000,000	$60,500,000	$66,550,000
Cost of goods sold (as % of revenue)	44%	42%	41%	40%
Cost of goods sold	–$22,000,000	–$23,100,000	–$24,805,000	–$26,620,000
Sales & marketing expenses (as % of revenue)	20%	20%	20%	20%
General & administrative expenses (as % of revenue)	6%	6%	6%	6%
Depreciation	–$20,000	–$20,000	–$20,000	–$20,000
Tax rate	35%	35%	35%	35%

Figure 13.16   All About HatWare's future business goals.

He also highlighted their three-year financial goals, going over the statements in Figure 13.16 to Figure 13.19.

From Figure 13.16, the CEO explained that, with IT's contribution, All About HatWare would aim to increase revenue as a result of sales to both wholesale and individual customers. With slight modifications to the final product, the company would aim to lower the cost of goods sold (as a percentage of revenue) over the following years. Meanwhile, due to the lower cost of marketing through mobile technology and social networks, All About HatWare also would be able to keep sales and marketing expenses (as a percentage of revenue) steady as they increased marketing efforts through these particular channels—and decreased efforts in costlier, traditional channels. These goals would ultimately translate into a higher operating profit and net income over the next three years, as demonstrated by Figure 13.17.

Pro Forma Income Statement

	Base Year	Year 1	Year 2	Year 3
Revenue	**$50,000,000**	**$55,000,000**	**$60,500,000**	**$66,550,000**
Raw materials	−3,000,000	−3,300,000	−3,630,000	−3,993,000
Direct labor costs	−19,000,000	−19,800,000	−21,175,000	−22,627,000
Cost of goods sold	**−$22,000,000**	**−$23,100,000**	**−$24,805,000**	**−$26,620,000**
Gross profit	**$28,000,000**	**$31,900,000**	**$35,695,000**	**$39,930,000**
Sales & marketing expenses	−10,000,000	−11,000,000	−12,100,000	−13,310,000
General & administrative expenses	−3,000,000	−3,300,000	−3,630,000	−3,993,000
Earnings before interest, taxes, depreciation & amortization	**$15,000,000**	**$17,600,000**	**$19,965,000**	**$22,627,000**
Depreciation expenses	−20,000	−20,000	−20,000	−20,000
Operating profit	**$14,980,000**	**$17,580,000**	**$19,945,000**	**$22,607,000**
Interest expense (Net)	0	0	0	0
Pretax income	**$14,980,000**	**$17,580,000**	**$19,945,000**	**$22,607,000**
Income taxes	−5,243,000	−6,153,000	−6,980,750	−7,912,450
Net income	**$9,737,000**	**$11,427,000**	**$12,964,250**	**$14,694,550**

Figure 13.17   Pro forma income statement.

Pro Forma Cash Flow Statement

	Base Year	Year 1	Year 2	Year 3
Net Income		$11,427,000	$12,964,250	$14,694,550
Depreciation		20,000	20,000	20,000
Changes in working capital				
Accounts receivable		3,287,671	−904,110	−994,521
Inventory		−230,137	−334,521	−358,027
Accounts payable		205,479	246,370	268,521
Cash from operating activities		$14,710,014	$11,991,990	$13,630,523
Capital expenditures		−50,000	−50,000	−50,000
Other investment		0	0	0
Cash from investing activities		−$50,000	−$50,000	−$50,000
Net borrowing		0	0	0
Dividends		0	0	0
Capital contributions		0	0	0
Cash from financing activities		0	0	0
Change in cash		$14,660,014	$11,941,990	$13,580,523

Figure 13.18   Pro forma cash flow.

Meanwhile, as conveyed in Figure 13.18, the CEO reiterated that the company would aim to continue generating similar levels of positive operating cash flow over the next several years. All About HatWare also would continue to hold extra cash on their balance sheet in case unforeseen external factors ever caused revenues to deteriorate and the company needed financial backup, as shown in Figure 13.19.

Pro Forma Balance Sheet

	Base Year	Year 1	Year 2	Year 3
Assets				
Cash and cash equivalents	$75,495,493	$90,155,507	$102,097,497	$115,678,019
Accounts receivable	12,328,767	9,041,096	9,945,205	10,939,726
Inventories	4,109,589	4,339,726	4,674,247	5,032,274
Total current assets	**$91,933,849**	**$103,536,329**	**$116,716,949**	**$131,650,019**
Property, plant, and equipment	230,000	260,000	290,000	320,000
Goodwill	80,000	80,000	80,000	80,000
Total assets	**$92,243,849**	**$103,876,329**	**$117,086,949**	**$132,050,019**
Liabilities				
Accounts payable	$2,506,849	$2,712,329	$2,958,699	$3,227,219
Debt	0	0	0	0
Total liabilities	**$2,506,849**	**$2,712,329**	**$2,958,699**	**$3,227,219**
Stockholders' equity				
Starting stockholders' equity	$80,000,000	$89,737,000	$101,164,000	$114,128,250
Net income	9,737,000	11,427,000	12,964,250	14,694,550
Dividends	0	0	0	0
Capital contributions	0	0	0	0
Stockholders' equity	**$89,737,000**	**$101,164,000**	**$114,128,250**	**$128,822,800**
Total liabilities & equity	**$92,243,849**	**$103,876,329**	**$117,086,949**	**$132,050,019**

Figure 13.19   Pro forma balance sheet.

13.5.2.2 Future Enterprise Business Processes

Meanwhile, Figure 13.20 conveys the essence of the direction that the CEO aimed to establish by announcing his objectives for All About HatWare's enterprise business processes:

- More emphasis on enterprise processes rather than on functional processes.
- Laser-like focus on executing the seamless integration of the software applications that would support these enterprise processes.

To understand how these software components could operate seamlessly behind the scenes, let us study Figure 13.21.

From this diagram, it appears as though all of these software components are connected via real-time interfaces, which would allow the company to speed up customers' orders and partners' supplies.

	Component				
Enterprise Processes	*Order*	*Distribution*	*Finance*	*Service*	*Facebook*
1. (Web) order to cash	x	x	x	x	
2. Order to bill	x	x	x	x	
3. Order to ship	x	x	x		
4. Like to order (on Facebook)	x	x	x	x	x

Figure 13.20 Different components of All About HotWare's future enterprise processes.

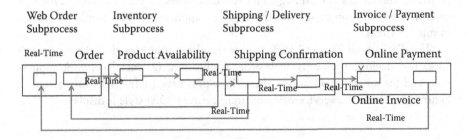

Figure 13.21 Future enterprise business process composition and optimization.

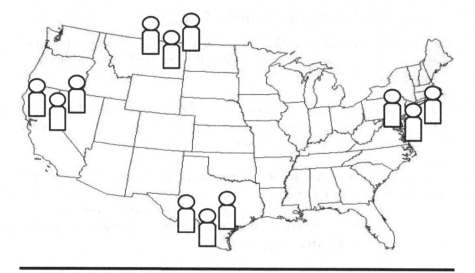

Figure 13.22   The new team distributed and Agile organization.

13.5.2.3 Future Team Structure

The CEO next sketched out the type of organizational structure he aimed to maintain at All About HatWare (Figure 13.22):

- Lean processes with no duplication of work
- Team collaboration and empowerment
- Team self-organization
- Lean and Agile business and IT organization, distributed throughout the United States

13.6 Future Enterprise IT Application Architecture

As part of the CEO's new strategy, Figure 13.23 shows an example of both the new enterprise business processes and the set of IT applications that would be created to support them.

The diagram in Figure 13.23 depicts the three priorities that the company's CEO had decided upon: (1) Web order application, (2) social network application, and (3) mobile application. These three priorities are further summarized in Figure 13.24, where a service-oriented architecture (SOA) style is displayed.

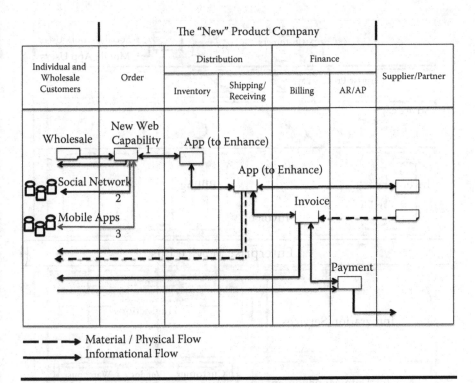

Figure 13.23 Future enterprise IT application architecture.

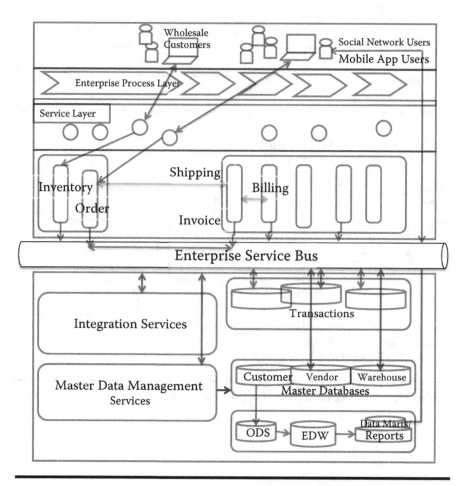

Figure 13.24 All About HatWare's service-oriented architecture (SOA).

13.7 Future Enterprise IT Data Architecture

Now that we have addressed the question of the future IT applications, let us move to the data side. As you already know, there are two aspects to the enterprise IT data architecture side:

1. Enterprise IT transactional data architecture
2. Enterprise IT BI/analytics data architecture

13.7.1 Future Enterprise IT Transactional Data Architecture

To avoid having problems with inconsistencies, All About HatWare's management also decided that data entities within its future transactional IT data architecture should be created and updated by only one single application, as indicated by the single "C" and "U" (for "create" and "update," respectively) found in the different cells within Figure 13.25.

Data	IT Applications						
	Order	Web Order	Mobile	Inventory	Shipping	Billing	AR/AP
Wholesale customers	C/U/D/R			R	R	R	R
Web individual customers		C/U/D/R		R	R		
Mobile customers			C/U/D/R	R	R		
Product, etc.							

Note: C = Create; U = Update; D = Delete; R = Read.

Figure 13.25   Data update by IT applications.

13.7.2 *Future Enterprise IT BI/Analytics Data Architecture*

As for the enterprise IT BI data architecture, Figure 13.26 is a reminder of what the current enterprise IT data architecture looked like. By closely observing this diagram, we can see that several "rogue" data feeds did not pass by the staging ETL (extract, transform, and load), as seen in #1 and #5. This is an occurrence that often created inconsistent numbers from report to report, even when it came from the same data fields.

Figure 13.27 portrays the future enterprise IT data architecture to be implemented with MDM (Master Data Management), which should help avoid the multiplication of data sources—and all of the resulting inconsistencies.

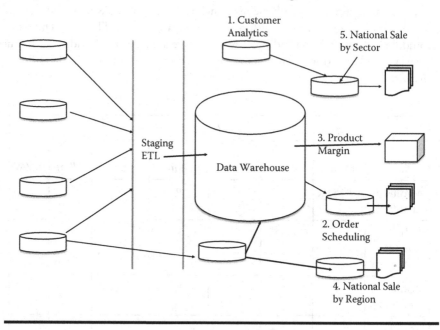

Figure 13.26   All About HatWare's current enterprise IT BI data architecture.

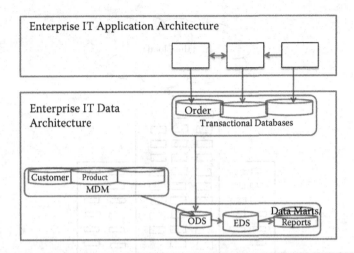

Figure 13.27   Enterprise IT data architecture with MDM.

13.8 Future Enterprise IT Infrastructure Architecture

Figure 13.28 demonstrates what has been decided in terms of All About HatWare's future infrastructure architecture: (1) cloud computing for development systems and (2) server consolidation for production.

Now that we have studied the current business and IT situation and the goals for the future business direction, let us overlay the former with the latter in order to identify the gaps that will ultimately form the foundation of the future IT roadmap.

13.9 Gaps in Enterprise Business Processes

According to Figure 13.29, we can see that there is a new enterprise process origi-nating from the Web for ordering, which did not previously allow individual cus-tomers to order the company's products online.

As part of the company's future goals, a new enterprise process has been created that will allow individual customers to order and to be billed via the Web. This requires a new subprocess for the ordering aspect, and also requires an enhance-ment of the inventory component and shipping component of this enterprise-wide process.

As long as we remember that software applications are mainly created to sup-port business processes, it will remain a rather straightforward task to identify the gaps in IT applications now that we have identified the gaps in business processes.

Figure 13.28 Moving the enterprise IT development to the cloud.

Enterprise Processes	Teams		
	Order Fulfillment	Distribution	Finance
1. Order	x To Enhance [gap]	x	x
2. Web order to cash	x	x	x
3. Web order to bill	x To Create [gap]	x To Enhance [gap]	
4. Order to ship	x To Create [gap]	x To Enhance [gap]	
5. Like to order (on Facebook)	x	x	

Figure 13.29 Gaps between current and future enterprise processes.

Enterprise Processes	Apps				
	Order	*Inventory*	*Shipping*	*Billing*	*AR/AP*
1. Order	x To Create [gap]	x		x	
2. Web order to cash	x		x	x	x
3. Web order to bill	x To Create [gap]	x To Enhance [gap]	x To Enhance [gap]		
4. Order to ship	x To Create [gap]	x To Enhance [gap]	x To Enhance [gap]		
5. Like to order (on Facebook)	x To Create [gap]	x To Enhance [gap]	x To Enhance [gap]		

Figure 13.30 IT application gaps.

13.10 Gaps in Enterprise IT Application Architecture

From Figure 13.30, it appears as though the main items listed are part of the gaps and, therefore, part of the future IT roadmap:

- Web order for individual customers
- Social network application
- Mobile software to facilitate sales to individual customers
- Use of an SOA architecture

13.11 Gaps in Enterprise IT Data Architecture

As we have already observed, having multiple software applications updating the same databases is undesirable. This is why it has since been acknowledged that a database entity should be updated by only one application, as shown in Figure 13.31.

Furthermore, Figure 13.31 provides an example with the shaded cells of two new data entities that have been added, along with the applications that are responsible for their creation and update.

In the same way that Figure 13.31 showed some new creation, Figure 13.32 shows with the shaded areas that the commercial company also had decided to set up a new MDM layer, in order to avoid data multiplication and, therefore, inconsistency.

	Current IT Applications					
Data	*Order*	*Web Order*	*Inventory*	*Shipping*	*Billing*	*AR/AP*
Wholesale customers	C/U					
Individual customers		C/U				
Order			C/U			
Product		C/U				
Etc.						

Note: C = Create; U = Update.

Figure 13.31 Gaps in enterprise IT data architecture.

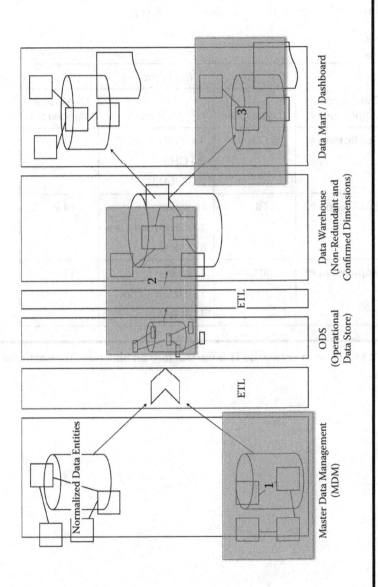

Figure 13.32   Gaps in enterprise IT data architecture.

13.12 Gaps in Enterprise IT Infrastructure Architecture

While the new direction is to move the development work to the cloud, Figure 13.33 and Figure 13.34 show the gaps within the company's enterprise IT infrastructure architecture, both in terms of transactional and BI capacity.

Transactional Applications	Infrastructure		
	(1) Database	*(2) Servers*	*(3) Network Bandwidth*
Application #1	5 GB	3 servers 2.4 GHz 2 GB RAM	T1
Application #2	2 TB	10 servers 2.4 GHz quad-core 8 GB RAM	Fiber
Application #3	100 GB	4 servers 3 GHz dual-core 4 GB RAM	T1

Figure 13.33   Gaps in enterprise IT infrastructure architecture: Transactional.

	Infrastructure		
BI Applications	*(1) Database*	*(2) Servers*	*(3) Network Bandwidth*
Application #1	10 GB	8 servers 2.4 GHz dual-core 2 GB RAM	T1
Application #2	5 GB	8 servers 2.4 GHz dual-core 2 GB RAM	T1
Application #3	700 GB	10 servers 2.4 GHz quad-core 4 GB RAM	Fiber
Application #4	6 GB	5 server 2.4 GHz 1 GB RAM	T1

Figure 13.34 Gaps in enterprise IT infrastructure architecture: Business intelligence.

13.13 IT Roadmap Components

Before we review the IT roadmap artifacts, let us first state what they are so that we may all be on the same page regarding All About HatWare's new business strategy and IT roadmap:

1. Business strategy, direction, and high level goals
2. Enterprise architecture
3. Business and technology initiatives prioritization
4. Timeline
5. IT budget

13.13.1 Business Strategy, Direction, and High-Level Goals

Now, to begin our review, Figure 13.35 is a high-level summary of what the CEO had stated in terms of business goals—along with a narrative of what he would like to see accomplished as part of All About HatWare's transformation:

- Transition from a semifinished product company to a finished product company.
- Sell not only to wholesale customers, but also to the professional individual customers.
- Leverage new mobile and social networks for marketing purposes.
- Save enterprise costs by working more closely with suppliers and partners while also leveraging technologies to the maximum.
- Review and enhance IT applications to better meet new business needs.
- Enhance customer value creation by more significantly leveraging enterprise business processes.

Business Goals Projections

Items	Base Year	Year 1	Year 2	Year 3
Annual revenue growth rate	8%	10%	10%	10%
Revenue	$50,000,000	$55,000,000	$60,5000,000	$66,550,000
Cost of goods sold (as % of revenue)	44%	42%	41%	40%
Cost of goods sold	–$22,000,000	–$23,100,000	–$24,805,000	–$26,620,000
Sales & marketing expenses (as % of revenue)	20%	20%	20%	20%
General & administrative expenses (as % of revenue)	6%	6%	6%	6%
Depreciation	–$20,000	–$20,000	–$20,000	–$20,000
Tax rate	35%	35%	35%	35%

Figure 13.35 All About HatWare's future business goals.

13.13.2 Enterprise Architecture

With regards to the enterprise architecture, Figure 13.36 is one-page summary of the architectural style of the new All About HatWare's IT application set. Rather than starting from scratch, All About HatWare's management made the decision to reuse most of their current IT applications while creating a new layer of services, known as the *service layer*. What management aimed to do was to get these applications to act as services that interact together in real-time to support some of the new enterprise business processes, without having to create all of these IT applications from scratch.

When we talk about real time within this new framework, we more specifically are referring to the service bus that should enable real-time data updates. This will help management analyze data as soon as they are updated, in order to make informed marketing and management decisions as part of their belief in the new analytics revolution.

Likewise, this new overall architecture also shows that there will be no more "rogue" data feeds. Instead, every single data feed will go through the ODS

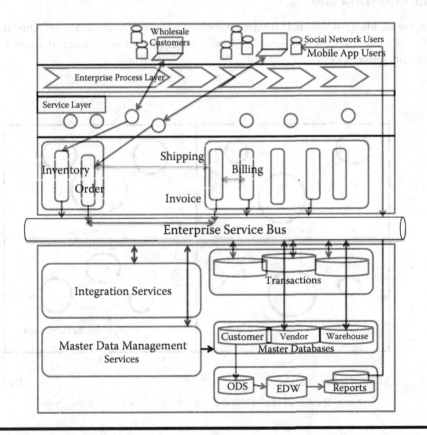

Figure 13.36   All About HatWare's service-oriented architecture (SOA).

(Operational Data Store) into the EDW (Enterprise Data Warehouse) from which data will be pulled to create data marts for analytical data analysis.

Now that we have seen the new enterprise architecture, it should go without saying that the transition to the new business strategy and enterprise architecture (EA) cannot happen overnight, but must be prioritized.

13.13.3 Business and Technology Initiatives Prioritization

We see this prioritization in Figure 13.37. To rank all of the new initiatives within the new IT roadmap, All About HatWare's management decided to place the initiatives in a matrix that guided them to start the roadmap by working on the "A" initiatives that were high in business value, but that also might have high associated risks. Thereafter, management would work on the "B" initiatives, then on the "C" initiatives, and, finally, on the "D" initiatives.

13.13.4 Timeline

In mentioning All About HatWare's prioritization, we also must discuss timeline. This is what is shown in Figure 13.38, which conveys an incremental delivery for the different tracks.

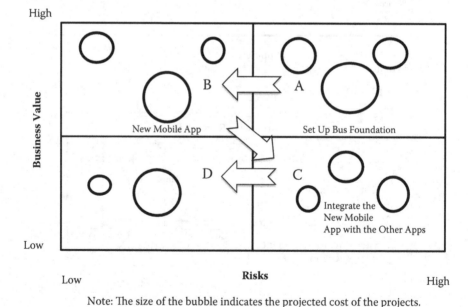

Note: The size of the bubble indicates the projected cost of the projects.

Figure 13.37　New IT applications prioritization matrix.

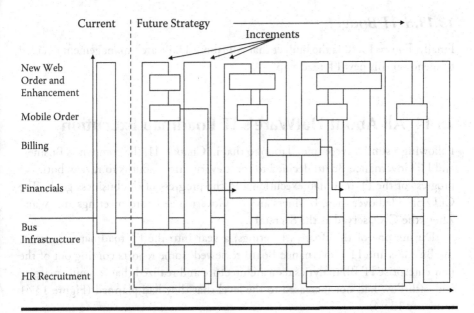

Figure 13.38 An Agile timeline.

While Figure 13.38 shows an Agile timeline, Figure 13.39 is a Lean view of the timeline. What they mean, respectively, is that while the former diagram shows the features being delivered incrementally, little by little, the latter shows that no single team will be asked to multitask.

Teams \ Timeline	January	February	March	April	May	June	Etc.
Web Order	☐☐ ☐ ☐	☐☐ ☐	☐☐ ☐☐ ☐				
Mobile Order			☐☐ ☐☐	☐☐ ☐	☐☐ ☐☐		
Billing		☐ ☐ ☐	☐☐ ☐	☐☐ ☐			
Financials			☐☐ ☐☐ ☐	☐☐ ☐☐	☐☐ ☐☐		

13.39 A Lean view of the roadmap timeline.

13.13.5 IT Budget

Finally, Figure 13.40 is the budget that All About HatWare's management decided to spend on this new IT roadmap.

13.14 All About HatWare's IT Roadmap Execution

Following a similar recommendation to that in Chapter 11, the company's Business and IT Governance Board decided to meet every three months to review both the progress of the IT roadmap execution and the progress of the business goals. The CEO presided over these Business and IT Governance Board meetings and Wang Zhou, the CIO, served as the Secretary.

During one of the Board's meetings, a year into the IT roadmap execution, the Business and IT Governance Board reviewed some reports coming out of the new enterprise IT BI/analytics data architecture and realized that revenue, margin, and cash flow had not increased to the level that they had planned (Figure 13.41 to Figure 13.44).

In other words, as conveyed by Figure 13.41, there was a large variance of −$10,000,000 between the revenue the company had expected for Year 1 and the actual revenue achieved. As a result, similar variances existed between planned and actual gross profit, operating profit, and net income.

As if management needed to be certain about the bad news, Figure 13.42, produced by using the new Enterprise Data Warehouse (EDW), further confirmed that their expectations for Year 1 revenue had not been met.

Similarly, Figure 13.43 confirmed that the company's profit margin also had been less than planned.

Finally, adding to the disappointing news, Figure 13.44 showed that cash flow had been less than planned as well.

Despite these rather pessimistic numbers, the production costs (Figure 13.45) seemed to have been contained or even reduced, considering the company's increase in production due to its diversification into the individual market.

This came as a relief to management as they realized that they would only have to deal with lackluster revenue—as opposed to both lackluster revenue and high enterprise cost at the same time.

While all of the preceding figures dealt with financials, Figure 13.46 provided an indication of the timeline, which seemed to suggest some kind of delay.

After further investigation into the issue of revenue, the CEO and the Business and IT Governance Board learned that one of the new IT applications was not very user-friendly and, for that reason, drove many customers away from the company's new hat product. Knowing this, the CEO, supported by the Board, then decided to increase the IT budget (as seen in Figure 13.47) in order to make its graphical user

IT Budget ($ in thousands)

1. Personnel expenses	**$2,000**
1.1 Contracting fees	500
1.2 Certification fees	50
1.3 Professional development	10
1.4 Business meetings	40
1.5 Travels and meals	10
1.6 Employee relocations	90
1.7 Health and life insurance	900
1.8 Employee tuition education assistance	250
1.9 Subscriptions and books	50
1.10 Others	100
2. Software and hardware expenses	**$4,000**
2.1 Software purchase	3,000
2.2 Others	1,000
3. Equipment expenses	**$6,000**
3.1 Rentals and leases	5,000
3.2 Repairs and maintenance	1,000
4. Telecom expenses	**$5,000**
4.1 Telephone	5,000
5. Office expenses	**$2,000**
5.1 Supplies (staplers, CDs, tape)	500
5.2 Postage	500
5.3 Janitorial services	1,000
Total	**$19,000**

Figure 13.40   IT roadmap budget.

Pro Forma Income Statement

	Base Year	Year 1	Year 1 Actual	Variance
Revenue	$50,000,000	$55,000,000	$45,000,000	–$10,000,000
Cost of goods sold	–$22,000,000	–$23,100,000	–$23,100,000	0
Gross profit	**$28,000,000**	**$31,900,000**	**$21,900,000**	**–$10,000,000**
Sales & marketing expenses	–10,000,000	–11,000,000	–7,900,000	3,100,000
General and administrative expenses	–3,000,000	–3,300,000	–3,200,000	100,000
Earnings before interest, taxes, depreciation & amortization	**$15,000,000**	**$17,600,000**	**$10,800,000**	**–$6,800,000**
Depreciation expenses	–20,000	–20,000	–20,000	0
Operating profit	**$14,980,000**	**$17,580,000**	**$10,780,000**	**–$6,800,000**
Interest expense (Net)	0	0	0	0
Pretax income	**$14,980,000**	**$17,580,000**	**$10,780,000**	**–$6,800,000**
Income taxes	–5,243,000	–6,153,000	–3,773,000	2,380,000
Net income	**$9,737,000**	**$11,427,000**	**$7,007,000**	**–$4,420,000**

Figure 13.41   Pro forma income statement.

interface (GUI) much more user-friendly, hoping that this would help increase the less than desirable level of revenue going forward.

Ultimately, despite all of these challenges during the execution of the new IT roadmap and new business direction, All About HatWare's unending commitment and dedication to the execution finally paid off. Subsequently, All About HatWare was able to overcome the challenges it had faced and thrived going forward, outgrowing its roots as a smaller, struggling family business to become a very successful commercial company traded publicly on the New York Stock Exchange.

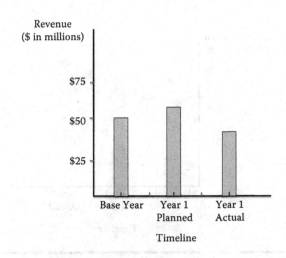

Figure 13.42 All About HatWare's revenue.

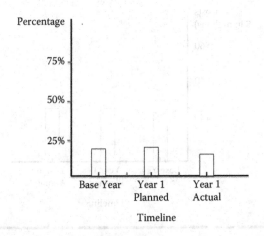

Figure 13.43 All About HatWare's profit margin.

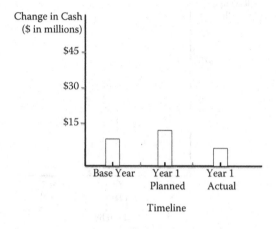

Figure 13.44 All About HatWare's cash flow.

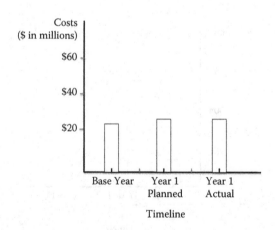

Figure 13.45 All About HatWare's production costs.

Tracks	Action Items	Timeline	Dependency	Status
1. Web Order Management	Action Item #1			△
2. Mobile Order	Action Item #1			▭
3. Billing	Action Item #1			◯
4. Financials	Action Item #1			◯
Etc.				

△ Green (On Track)

◯ Red (Late)

▭ Yellow (Some Concern)

Figure 13.46   IT roadmap status by tracks.

IT Budget ($ in thousands)

1. Personnel Expenses	$4,000
1.1 Contracting fees	3,000
1.2 Certification fees	50
1.3 Professional development	10
1.4 Business meetings	40
1.5 Travels and meals	10
1.6 Employee relocations	90
1.7 Health and life insurance	400
1.8 Employee tuition education assistance	250
1.9 Subscriptions and books	50
1.10 Others	100
2. Software and hardware expenses	**$5,000**
2.1 Software purchase	3,000
2.2 Others	2,000
3. Equipment expenses	**$9,000**
3.1 Rentals and leases	5,000
3.2 Repairs and maintenance	4,000
4. Telecom expenses	**$5,000**
4.1 Telephone	5,000
5. Office expenses	**$4,000**
5.1 Supplies (staplers, CDs, tape)	2,500
5.2 Postage	500
5.3 Janitorial services	1,000
Total	**$27,000**

Figure 13.47   Revised IT roadmap budget.

Chapter 14

Case Study 2: Nonprofit Case Study: US Against Illiteracy

US Against Illiteracy is a nonprofit association that aims to fight against child illiteracy and has an especially strong focus on the New York City area.

As with the previous case study, we will retrace the same diagram that we followed in Chapter 7, shown again in Figure 14.1, to help us go through the process by which this nonprofit association determined its business strategy and created a technology roadmap that would support it.

Like in the first case study, we will discuss the following aspects of US Against Illiteracy in this second case study:

14.1:   Current Enterprise Business Architecture
14.2:   Current Enterprise IT Application Architecture
14.3:   Current Enterprise IT Data Architecture
14.4:   Current Enterprise IT Infrastructure Architecture
14.5:   Future Business Strategy and Its New Enterprise Business Architecture
14.6:   Future Enterprise IT Application Architecture
14.7:   Future Enterprise IT Data Architecture
14.8:   Future Enterprise IT Infrastructure Architecture
14.9:   Gaps in Enterprise Business Processes
14.10: Gaps in Enterprise IT Application Architecture
14.11: Gaps in Enterprise IT Data Architecture

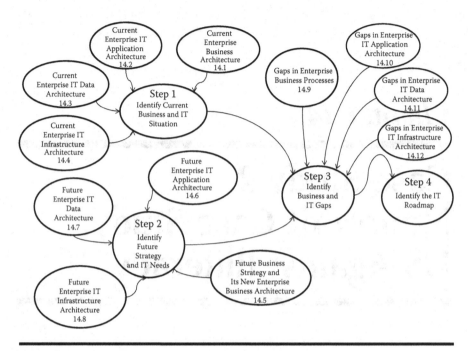

Figure 14.1   Detailed IT roadmap formulation process.

14.1 Current Enterprise Business Architecture

14.1.1 Business Goals

Like many other small-scale nonprofits, US Against Illiteracy began as a very simple charity with an altruistic mission. It aimed to raise donations from US residents in order to implement literacy programs that would bring more books to children throughout the nation.

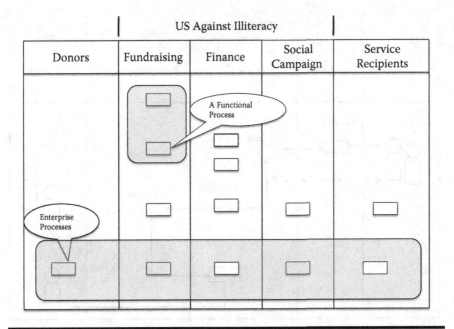

Figure 14.2 **Business processes within US Against Illiteracy.**

14.1.2 Business Processes

Though hard to believe, US Against Illiteracy's only enterprise business process (in other words, the only process that cut across the different teams) was the one by which a donor makes a donation and receives a receipt for the money donated. This process is depicted in detail in Figure 14.2.

14.1.3 Team Structure

The organization itself began as a rather simple structure, organized around classic functions, such as donation fundraising, finance, and social campaigns, all based in New York City.

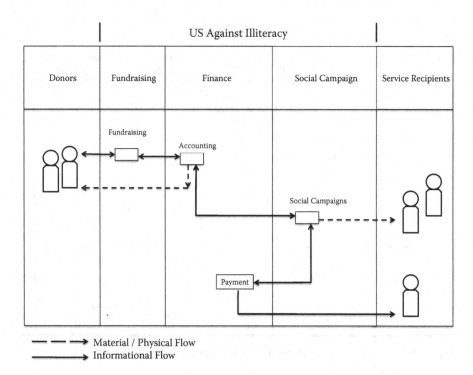

Figure 14.3   Current enterprise IT application architecture.

14.2 Current Enterprise IT Application Architecture

As shown in Figure 14.3, several in-house software applications supported the various business processes at US Against Illiteracy.

However, as US Against Illiteracy continued to grow in scale, the in-house applications became less useful, leveraging technologies that had since disappeared from the market.

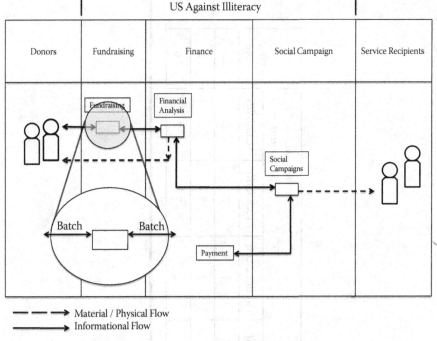

Figure 14.4   Current enterprise IT application architecture.

Frequently, these applications were not well integrated together and, in addition, many of the interfaces were batch interfaces, as shown in Figure 14.4.

Unsurprisingly, a more in-depth assessment reveals that some of these applications either required a face-lift or needed to be completely replaced by another application, especially when you come to realize that they provided critical support to some of the most important business processes of the association (see Figure 14.5 and Figure 14.6).

Applications	Score					Minimum: 1 Maximum: 5	
	Business Alignment	Maintainability	Architecture	Modularity	Scalability		Average Score
1. Fundraising	2	2	1	3	2		2.0
2. Financial Analysis	2	2	2	2	2		2.0
3. Social Campaign	2	2	2	2	2		2.0

Figure 14.5 Current IT transactional application assessment.

Processes	IT Applications			
	Fundraising	*Finance*	*Social Campaign*	*Etc.*
Receipt on Donation	×	×		
Special Event		×	×	
Recipient Analysis			×	
Etc.				

Figure 14.6   Business processes as supported by IT applications.

While the previous diagrams focused on the transactional applications, Figure 14.7 and Figure 14.8 are geared towards the business intelligence (BI) area.

14.3 Current Enterprise IT Data Architecture

Assessing the current enterprise IT data architecture of US Against Illiteracy, we can see that the different databases had grown to contain a lot of inconsistencies, resulting from the fact that many applications could update the same data entity.

14.3.1 Enterprise IT Transactional Data Architecture

The enterprise IT transactional data architecture resembled Figure 14.9.

14.3.2 Enterprise IT BI Data Architecture

Meanwhile, the enterprise IT BI data architecture resembled Figure 14.10. There appeared to be a risk of inconsistency in the BI that needed to be fixed.

Applications	Score					Minimum: 1 Maximum: 5	
	Business Alignment	Maintainability	Architecture	Modularity	Scalability		Average Score
1. Financial Analysis	2	5	3	1	1		2.4
2. Marketing Analysis	2	2	2	2	2		2.0
3. Campaign Analysis	2	2	2	2	2		2.0

Figure 14.7   US Against Illiteracy's current enterprise IT BI application architectural assessment.

	IT Applications			
Processes	Fundraising	Finance	Social Campaign	Etc.
Receipt on Donation	×	×		
Financial Analysis			×	
Social Campaign		×	×	

Figure 14.8   Business processes as supported by IT BI applications.

	Current IT Applications			
Data	Fundraising	Finance	Social Campaign	Etc.
Donor	C/R/U/D	U/R		
Donation	C/U	U/R		
Receipt	C/U	C/U		
Campaign		R/U	R/U	
Recipient		R/U	R/U	

Note: C = Create; R = Read; U = Update; D = Delete.

Figure 14.9   IT data architecture by current transactional applications.

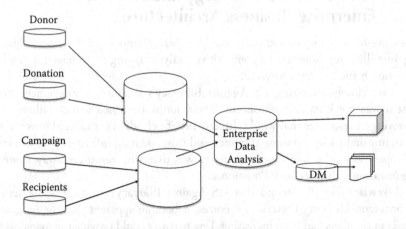

Figure 14.10   Current IT BI data architecture.

Transactional Applications	Infrastructure		
	(1) Database	(2) Servers	(3) Network Bandwidth
Application #1	1 GB	1 server 2.4 GHz 2 GB RAM	T1
Application #2	2 GB	1 server 2.4 GHz quad-core 8 GB RAM	T1
Application #3	2 GB	1 server 3 GHz dual-core 4 GB RAM	T1

Figure 14.11   Current enterprise IT infrastructure architecture: Transactional.

14.4 Current Enterprise IT Infrastructure Architecture

Similar to other start-ups, especially within the social sector, US Against Illiteracy's current enterprise IT infrastructure was not as large and complex as a large commercial organization. Figure 14.11 and Figure 14.12 alone sum up what the association currently had.

14.5 Future Business Strategy and Its New Enterprise Business Architecture

Growing increasingly concerned about their status among similar nonprofits, US Against Illiteracy conducted a competitive analysis, trying to understand in which direction it should move forward.

After closely analyzing US Against Illiteracy's situation, management found that it was not internally consistent. Their nonprofit aimed to fight illiteracy by investing in resources that would directly benefit children's reading. However, due to an unusually high amount of money and time spent on infrastructure and internal operations, the resulting inefficiency was diverting resources away from the organization's ultimate social mission.

Likewise, they also found that US Against Illiteracy's strategy was externally inconsistent. Utilizing Porter's Five Forces, it became apparent that the bargaining power of suppliers had been increasing. Few partners could provide the materials and

BI Applications	Infrastructure		
	(1) Database	(2) Servers	(3) Network Bandwidth
1. Financial Analysis	10 GB	1 server 2.4 GHz dual-core 2 GB RAM	T1
2. Marketing Analysis	5 GB	2 servers 2.4 GHz dual-core 2 GB RAM	T1
3. Campaign Analysis	700 GB	2 servers 2.4 GHz quad-core 2 GB RAM	T1

Figure 14.12 Current enterprise IT infrastructure architecture: Business intelligence.

supplies that the organization needed to fully run its nonprofit operations; these partners could therefore negotiate against US Against Illiteracy as needed—though they had fortunately previously held back, out of goodwill towards the children. It also was apparent that some of the organization's constituents wielded far too much leverage. The organization had failed to diversify its sources of income and, thus, relied on constant contributions from the same few generous donors of money and time.

On the other hand, the bargaining power of service and product recipients was not problematic. After all, the children selected to benefit from the organization's resources were rather grateful for the support US Against Illiteracy provided. Nonetheless, after examining the other aspects of Porter's Five Forces, the threat of new entrants and substitutes were never-ending. New charities with similar aims continued to form and vie for the same donation dollars. US Against Illiteracy found that it also had to compete with substitutes, such as other nonprofits like museums with different missions to which institutions and individuals could donate money.

Regarding other organizations as competitors for donation, US Against Illiteracy feared that its competitors had found ways to improve their service or product while also reducing their own cost structure compared to US Against Illiteracy. In fact, after conducting a relative cost analysis, US Against Illiteracy found that the costs of software application development and maintenance had indeed become more expensive at its own organization than at its competitors. As a result, US Against Illiteracy decided it would need to streamline its software development and reduce associated costs.

		Current	Market Penetration	Partial Product/ Service Diversification	Product Development
Market					
	New		Market Development	Partial Market Diversification	Diversification

	Current	Modified	New
		Product/Service	

Figure 14.13   Product–Market Growth Directions Matrix for US Against Illiteracy.

After developing a first cut of its Strategy Blade, US Against Illiteracy's strengths and weaknesses became even more apparent. The various parts of the Blade were not working well together to drive the organization's purpose of fighting illiteracy. Many of the choices the organization had made in activities had rendered them mediocre at best. However, the continued popularity of the organization reassured the management team that they were in the right space and that they simply needed to diversify their sources of income in order to avoid depending on only a few for their survival. To this effect and in order to successfully reduce the charity's reliance on a few large donations, the organization decided they would need to develop modified products and services that could generate the remaining amount of income required by the nonprofit. These products and services would, of course, continue to relate to the organization's ultimate mission of improving children's literacy rates.

As they began to investigate this, it became increasingly apparent that US Against Illiteracy should move to partially diversify its market to also target individual donors. Thus, these partially modified products that they hoped to launch would need to appeal both to its current market of institutional donors and this new market of individual donors. One idea that came from its team's brainstorming involved offering pay-per-view children's books, whereby children could volunteer to write "novels" that would be available for online purchase. This idea stemmed from the nonprofit's current offering of pay-per-view children's poems, which had drawn ecstatic feedback from supporters requesting even more to read. The Product–Market Growth Directions Matrix, as seen in Figure 14.13, shows the direction of this expansion, which turned out to be remarkably creative. We will discuss this in further detail later.

But before we move ahead, below is a summary of the conclusion that management had come up with for the association's new business direction, including a list of three-year financial goals.

Revenues	Base Year	Year 1	Year 2	Year 3
Special Events	$80,000	$80,000	$80,000	$80,000
Sponsorships of illiterate children (to be obtained from the IT roadmap that supports the future business direction)	35,000	40,000	45,000	50,000
Sales of books written by children (to be obtained from the IT roadmap that supports the future business direction)	100,000	150,000	175,000	185,000
Fundraising campaign from institutional donors	240,000	240,000	240,000	240,000
Fundraising campaign from individual donors	75,000	75,000	75,000	75,000
Government grant	25,000	25,000	50,000	50,000
Total revenue	**$555,000**	**$610,000**	**$665,000**	**$680,000**

Figure 14.14   Revenue projections.

14.5.1 Future Goals and Direction

Though the nonprofit was still new, the young management team truly believed in its mission. For this reason, the team had arrived at very aggressive financial goals, to which they firmly believed technology should make a large contribution.

Along with the financial goals found in Figure 14.14, the following encompassed the team's ideas for the organization's future business direction and IT roadmap:

■ Pursue aggressive growth, harnessed by celebrity endorsements and sponsorships of illiterate children.

■ Offer "novels" written by children that can be purchased online by readers; the money from sales would be used to drive additional social campaigns in those children's neighborhoods.

■ Leverage mobile applications to expand audience reach and build social awareness.

Figure 14.15   US Against Illiteracy's new virtual and distributed organization.

14.5.2 Future Team Structure

In support of this new expansion, the management team also had envisioned the organization's team structure as a remote Lean organization, with no duplication of work (Figure 14.15).

14.5.3 Future Enterprise Business Processes

Next, the management team took the opportunity to come up with some new enterprise business processes which they thought should bring more value to their constituents and donors, trying to optimize them as much as possible, as shown in Figures 14.16 and 14.17.

As for Figure 14.18, it shows an example of a detailed decomposition of some of the association's new enterprise business processes interacting together as part of a composition.

Enterprise Processes	Description	Applications		
		Fundraising	*Finance*	*Social Campaign*
1. Enterprise Process #1	Allows donors to donate to children residing specifically in certain neighborhoods	×	×	×
2. Enterprise Process #2	Publishes children's own novels along with pictures for pay per view		×	×
3. Enterprise Process #3	Allows people to buy and read a child's book on the Web and mobile phone	×	×	

Figure 14.16 Some of US Against Illiteracy's future enterprise processes.

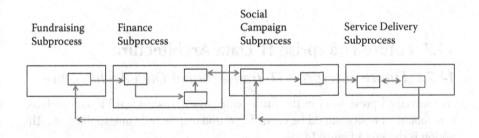

Fundraising Subprocess   Finance Subprocess   Social Campaign Subprocess   Service Delivery Subprocess

Figure 14.17   Future enterprise business process composition and optimization.

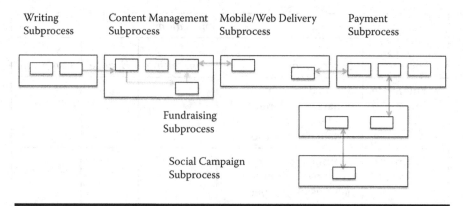

Figure 14.18 A more detailed enterprise business process.

14.6 Future Enterprise IT Application Architecture

As briefly mentioned from our previous discussion, the following is a summary of some of the new applications that would support the new enterprise business processes, including:

- Donations to a specific neighborhood's children
- Web publication of children's books
- Web- and mobile-based reading and payment of novels

These applications can be found in Figure 14.19.

14.7 Future Enterprise IT Data Architecture

14.7.1 Future Enterprise IT Transactional Data Architecture

As mentioned previously, in the future enterprise transactional IT data architecture, one data entity should be created and updated by only one application. This notion is shown in Figure 14.20.

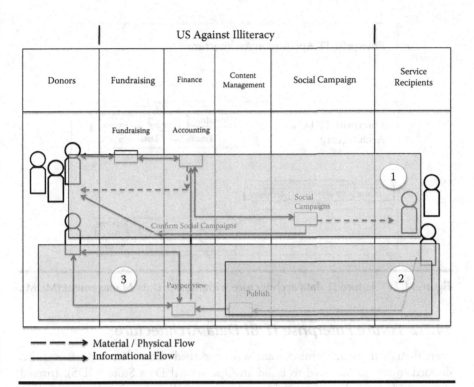

Figure 14.19   Future enterprise IT application architecture.

Data	IT Applications					
	Fundraising	Finance	Social Campaign	Special Donate	Publish	Pay per View
Donor	C/U					
Donation		C/U				
Receipt		C/U				
Campaign			C/U			
Recipient				C/U		
Author					C/U	
Book					C/U	
Payment						C/U
Reader, etc.						C/U

Note: C = Create; U = Update.

Figure 14.20   Future IT data architecture by IT applications.

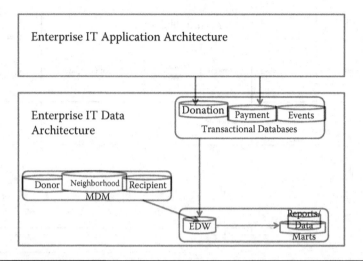

Figure 14.21   Future IT data architecture with Master Data Management (MDM).

14.7.2 Future Enterprise IT BI Data Architecture

Even though the management team was concerned about data consistency, they decided to forego the need to build an Operational Data Store (ODS). Instead, they would store what they might need to report directly in an Enterprise Data Warehouse (EDW) (Figure 14.21).

Transactional Applications	Infrastructure		
	1 Database	2 Servers	3 Network Bandwidth
Application #1 Enhancement to the current donation application	1 GB	1 server 2.4 GHz 2 GB RAM	T1
Application #2 Web publication of children's books	4 GB	1 server 2.4 GHz Quad-core 12 GB RAM	T1
Application #3 Web- and mobile-based reading and payment of novels	6 GB	1 server 3 GHz Dual-core 14 GB RAM	T1

Figure 14.22   Future enterprise IT infrastructure architecture: Transactional.

BI Application	Infrastructure		
	1 Database	2 Servers	3 Network Bandwidth
1. Online Marketing Analysis	20 GB	1 server 2.4 GHz Dual-core 2 GB RAM	T1

Figure 14.23   Future enterprise IT infrastructure architecture: Business intelligence.

14.8 Future Enterprise IT Infrastructure Architecture

The focus of US Against Illiteracy's future enterprise IT infrastructure roadmap (Figure 14.22 and Figure 14.23) would be on (1) upgrading servers and (2) server backup.

Enterprise Processes	Teams/Applications				
	Fundraising	Distribution	Purchase	Social Campaign	Finance
Donate	X	X			X
Donate to specific neighborhoods	X To Enhance [Gap]	X To Enhance [Gap]		C To Create [Gap]	X To Enhance [Gap]
Web publishing			X To Enhance [Gap]	X To Enhance [Gap]	
Web reading	X To Enhance [Gap]	X To Enhance [Gap]	X To Enhance [Gap]		X To Enhance [Gap]
Web payment	X To Enhance [Gap]	X To Enhance [Gap]		X To Enhance [Gap]	X To Enhance [Gap]
Mobile publishing			C To Create [Gap]	C To Create [Gap]	
Mobile reading	C To Create [Gap]	C To Create [Gap]	C To Create [Gap]		C To Create [Gap]
Mobile payment	C To Create [Gap]	C To Create [Gap]		C To Create [Gap]	C To Create [Gap]

Note: X = Current situation; C = Create.

Figure 14.24 Gaps in enterprise business processes.

14.9 Gaps in Enterprise Business Processes

As expected, US Against Illiteracy laid the future enterprise business processes over the current enterprise business processes. In doing this, they were able to identify the gaps that should drive the future IT roadmap.

To this effect, the association would need to facilitate the following enterprise business processes, as seen in Figure 14.24:

1. Donations to a specific neighborhood's children
2. Allowing children to write and publish their own novels on the association's web apps
3. Web- or mobile-based reading and online mobile payments

14.10 Gaps in Enterprise IT Application Architecture

14.10.1 Enterprise IT Transactional Applications

US Against Illiteracy next identified that it would require some new application types for enterprise IT transactional applications, as seen in Figure 14.25.

Enterprise Processes	Teams/Applications				
	Fundraising	Finance	Online Content	Social Campaign	Service Delivery
Donate	X	X			X
Donate to specific neighborhoods	X To Enhance [Gap]	X To Enhance [Gap]		C To Create [Gap]	X To Enhance [Gap]
Web publishing			X To Enhance [Gap]	X To Enhance [Gap]	
Web reading	X To Enhance [Gap]	X To Enhance [Gap]	X To Enhance [Gap]		X To Enhance [Gap]
Web payment	X To Enhance [Gap]	X To Enhance [Gap]		X To Enhance [Gap]	X To Enhance [Gap]
Mobile publishing			C To Create [Gap]	C To Create [Gap]	
Mobile reading	C To Create [Gap]	C To Create [Gap]	C To Create [Gap]		C To Create [Gap]
Mobile payment	C To Create [Gap]	C To Create [Gap]		C To Create [Gap]	C To Create [Gap]

Note: X = Current situation; C = Create.

Figure 14.25 Gaps in enterprise IT transactional applications.

Enterprise Processes	Applications				
	Fundraising	Distribution	Purchase	Social Campaign	Finance
1. Online Marketing Analysis	C To Create [Gap]	C To Create [Gap]			C To Create [Gap]

Figure 14.26 Gaps in enterprise IT BI applications.

14.10.2 Enterprise IT BI Applications

Meanwhile, BI applications of US Against Illiteracy would require online marketing analysis BI. Figure 14.26 details specific gaps in BI applications for the association.

14.11 Gaps in Enterprise IT Data Architecture

While Figure 14.27 shows the gaps in terms of transactional databases, Figure 14.28 shows that, to meet the new business strategy needs, the new data feeds into the data warehouse would come from two new transactional applications: the Publish app and the Finance app, respectively.

14.12 Gaps in Enterprise IT Infrastructure Architecture

The gaps in enterprise IT infrastructure architecture are straightforward to identify. As a financial summary, Figure 14.29 and Figure 14.30 show the budget required to cover both the gaps and the needs of the current operations.

Data / IT Applications	Fundraising	Finance	Social Campaign	Special Donate	Publish	Pay per View
Donor	X To Enhance [Gap]					
Donation	X	C To Create [Gap]				
Receipt	X	X To Enhance [Gap]				
Campaign		X	X To Enhance [Gap]			
Recipient			X	C To Create [Gap]		
Author					C To Create [Gap]	
Book					C To Create [Gap]	
Payment						C To Create [Gap]
Reader, etc.						C To Create [Gap]

Notes: X = Current Situation; C = Create

Figure 14.27 Gaps in IT data architecture by transactional applications.

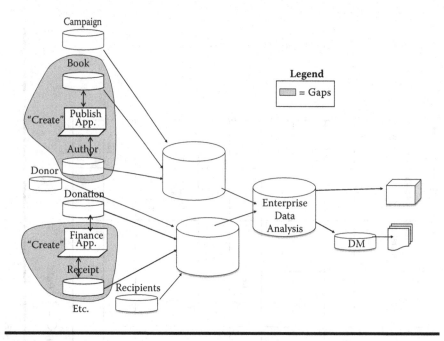

Figure 14.28 Gaps in IT data architecture due to the new transactional applications.

Future Server Need Estimate

SQL Servers:	$9,000
Server Upgrades:	$6,250
Domain Controller	$3,150
Backup Controller:	$5,000
Firewall/Internet Protection:	$4,000
Total:	$27,400

Figure 14.29 Budget to meet future server needs, including gaps and current operations.

Future Hardware Estimate

Hardware	
Laptops	$23,000
Miscellaneous	$450
Printers	
HP Desk Jet	$750
HP Laser Jet	$1,000
Equipment	
Network Analyzer	$5,004
Desktop Hardware	
Backup Desktop Computer	$2,252
Total	**$32,456**

Figure 14.30   Budget to meet future hardware needs, including gaps and current operations.

14.13 IT Roadmap Components

Before we review the IT roadmap artifacts in the following pages, let us first restate what they are so as to remain on the same page regarding US Against Illiteracy's new business strategy and IT roadmap:

1. Business strategy, direction, and high level goals
2. Enterprise architecture
3. Business and technology initiatives prioritization
4. Timeline
5. IT budget

Revenues	Base Year	Year 1	Year 2	Year 3
Special events	$80,000	$80,000	$80,000	$80,000
Revenue from sponsorships of illiterate children (to be obtained from the IT roadmap that supports the future business direction)	35,000	40,000	45,000	50,000
Revenue from the sale of books written by children (to be obtained from the IT roadmap that supports the future business direction)	100,000	150,000	175,000	185,000
Fundraising campaign from institutional donors	240,000	240,000	240,000	240,000
Fundraising campaign from individual donors	75,000	75,000	75,000	75,000
Government grant	25,000	25,000	50,000	50,000
Total revenue	**$555,000**	**$610,000**	**$665,000**	**$680,000**

Figure 14.31   Revenue projections.

14.13.1 Business Strategy, Direction, and Goals

The management team had arrived at very aggressive financial goals, to which they firmly believed that technology should be able to make a large contribution.

Along with the financial goals found in Figure 14.31, the following encompassed the team's ideas for the organization's future business direction and IT roadmap:

■ Pursue aggressive growth, harnessed by celebrity endorsements and sponsorships of illiterate children.
■ Offer "novels" written by children that can be purchased online by readers; and the money from sales would be used to drive additional social campaigns in those children's neighborhoods.
■ Leverage mobile applications to expand audience reach and build social awareness.

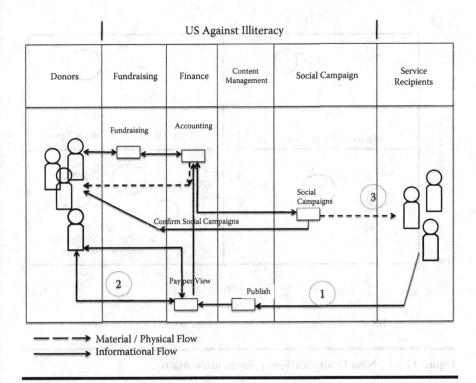

Figure 14.32 Future enterprise IT application architecture.

14.13.2 Enterprise Architecture

With regards to the enterprise architecture, Figure 14.32 summarizes the architectural style of the new US Against Illiteracy IT application set.

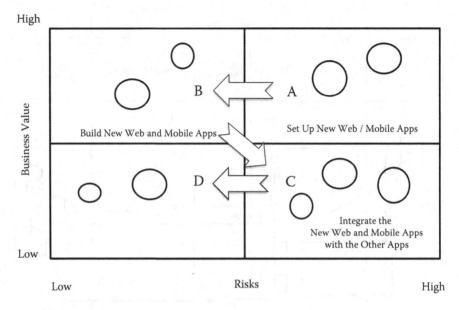

Note: The size of the bubble indicates the projected cost of the projects.

Figure 14.33   New IT applications prioritization matrix.

14.13.3 Business and Technology Initiatives Prioritization

To rank all of the new initiatives within the new IT roadmap, US Against Illiteracy's management decided to start the roadmap by working on the "A" initiatives as shown in Figure 14.33. Next, management would work on the "B" initiatives, then on the "C" initiatives, and finally, on the "D" initiatives.

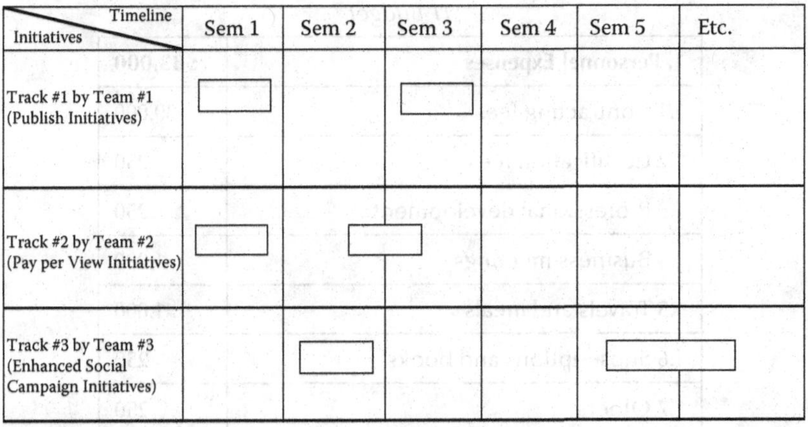

Initiatives \ Timeline	Sem 1	Sem 2	Sem 3	Sem 4	Sem 5	Etc.
Track #1 by Team #1 (Publish Initiatives)	▭		▭			
Track #2 by Team #2 (Pay per View Initiatives)	▭	▭				
Track #3 by Team #3 (Enhanced Social Campaign Initiatives)		▭			▭	

Figure 14.34   A Lean view of the IT roadmap timeline.

14.13.4 Timeline

In mentioning US Against Illiteracy's prioritization, we also must discuss timeline. A Lean view of the roadmap timeline is shown in Figure 14.34.

14.13.5 IT Budget

The budget supporting the above roadmap and timeline is given in Figure 14.35.

IT Budget

1. Personnel Expenses	**$83,000**
1.1 Contracting fees	80,000
1.2 Certification fees	250
1.3 Professional development	250
1.4 Business meetings	1,000
1.5 Travels and meals	1,000
1.6 Subscriptions and books	250
1.7 Others	250
2. Software and Hardware Expenses	**$52,800**
2.1 Software purchase	10,000
2.2 Others	42,800
3. Equipment Expenses	**$18,056**
3.1 Rentals and leases	17,056
3.2 Repairs and maintenance	1,000
4. Telecom Expenses	**$2,000**
4.1 Telephone	2,000
5. Office Expenses	**$1,800**
5.1 Supplies (staplers, CDs, tape)	1,000
5.2 Postage	200
5.3 Janitorial services	600
Total	**$157,656**

Figure 14.35   IT roadmap budget.

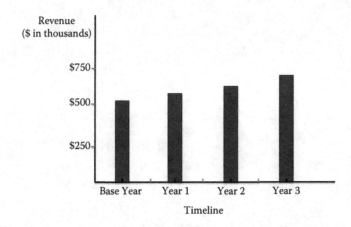

Figure 14.36 US Against Illiteracy revenue projections.

14.14 US Against Illiteracy's IT Roadmap Execution

In comparison with other nonprofits, US Against Illiteracy, as a relatively small organization, is similar in many ways to a start-up. To this effect, their executive review is somewhat less formal, but also more regular than in the case of All About HatWare.

With the launch of the IT roadmap execution at US Against Illiteracy, the Business and IT Governance Board was quite happy that everything was going as planned, both in terms of IT spending and revenue projections, as shown in Figure 14.36.

All in all, US Against Illiteracy's consistent efforts led to successful growth, and the nonprofit association continued to thrive in its social mission.

Appendix A: The 10 Questions an IT Leader Should Ask His or Her CEO or Board Members

1. What business do you think we are in?
2. What is our mission?
3. What is your vision and goals for our business for the next 10 years, five years, three years, and next year?
4. Who are our competitors?
5. What do our competitors do that keeps you awake at night?
6. What do you think we should do to keep our customers happy?
7. What do you think we should do to expand our market share or to generate more revenue?
8. What do you think we should do to increase our value proposition and make us unique?
9. What are the five things you like the most about IT?
10. What are the five things you dislike the most about IT?

Appendix B: The 10 Questions the CEO or Board Member Should Ask His or Her IT Leader

1. What can you do to keep our customers or constituents?
2. What can you do to expand our customers or constituents?
3. What can you do to make buying or receiving our products or services easy?
4. What can you do to make doing business or working with us easy?
5. What can you do to reduce our enterprise cost?
6. What can you do to simplify or make our enterprise business processes leaner and more effective?
7. What can you do to increase our teams' productivity?
8. What can you do to make our products and/or services unique and different from that of our competitors?
9. What can you do to prevent our competitors from surpassing us?
10. What can you do to help innovate our products and/or services?

Appendix C: Leveraging Social Media for Business Strategy

Leveraging Social Media for Business Strategy and IT Roadmap

Social media has become an increasingly powerful tool that can be leveraged toward viral marketing, public relations, and customer service at a low cost. Therefore, developing a carefully thought out social strategy is essential to making certain your organization achieves maximum effectiveness.

With the recent advent of social networks, such as Facebook, Twitter, and Google+, your organization should leverage these technological tools to bolster its business strategy, thereby broadening its reach, expanding its visibility, and developing stronger customer or constituent relationships.

As customers or constituents demonstrate increased brand loyalty across these social networks, organizations can exponentially expand their customer or constituent base through the resulting network effects. Fans devoted to an organization's product or service have the ability to draw in their friends, family, and colleagues by personally vouching for the brands they like on these online networks. In turn, their friends, family, and colleagues may suggest their own recommendations to their contacts, creating a word-of-mouth effect and reinforcing the use of a product or service across a connected web of people.

It is admittedly difficult to calculate the return on investment (ROI) directly resulting from an organization's social media efforts, but what is indisputable is the lasting impact that an effective social media strategy can have on driving greater commitment from customers or constituents. These customers or constituents, thereafter, may possess the motivation to promote a product or service at a much lower cost and with a much wider reach than an organization doing so alone.

229

Despite all the aforementioned benefits, employing social networks incorrectly can create a boomerang effect. Therefore, it is imperative that an organization thoroughly thinks through all of the effects that may follow the implementation of its strategy.

New Media Channel

Viral Marketing

With the types of technology now available, organizations should no longer aim to "reach" customers or constituents in order to "encourage" the use of their product or service as was once deemed sufficient via traditional media outlets like television and radio. Innovation among social platforms themselves offers organizations an array of tools to interact and connect with customers or constituent in unique and creative ways.

Facebook, for example, allows organizations to register for a profile page. On these pages, organizations may post announcements regarding new products or services, rewarding their most loyal users with up-to-date information or insider news. In these instances, users can click the "Like" button below these announcements in order to publicly display their approval and support to their own network of friends on Facebook. Organizations also may post new promotions, contests, or sweepstakes to engage users. To gain more Facebook fans, organizations may then employ the "Like-Gating" technique, which prevents a user from entering a certain contest or sweepstake unless the user first "Likes" the organization's page. Additionally, organizations can drive participation from fans by genuinely inviting and reacting to fans' comments on the page or by offering incentives to fans that successfully refer others to certain promotions, thereby enhancing the word-of-mouth effect. Collectively, these mechanisms can enhance the viral nature of organizations' marketing campaigns on Facebook.

Twitter, on the other hand, utilizes different mechanisms to drive the same viral effects as Facebook. Users can post their thoughts (known as "tweeting") and express a positive or negative sentiment to their network of followers. In turn, these followers may utilize the "Retweet" button in order to repeat the published thought to their own networks, crediting the user from which the post originated. Thus, a web of connectivity is created as users tweet and retweet each other's musings.

For a company, it can be extraordinarily beneficial to build a strong base of followers by tweeting and retweeting target users' thoughts, an action that invites communication between the company and these prospective customers. The greater the number of followers a company can attain through this method, the greater the likelihood that the company's posts will spread through word-of-mouth as followers share the announcements with their own, often like-minded, networks. Companies that effectively utilize Twitter to communicate with their customers are able to strengthen the commitment from their client base over time.

Recently launched TV shows provide a unique example of how you might effectively leverage Twitter to increase viewership loyalty. NBC's *The Voice* has its celebrity judges tweet their reactions to singers performing onstage. Each of these celebrity judges, in turn, has millions of loyal fans. When fans notice tweets from their favorite celebrities continually referring to *The Voice*, they are more compelled to watch in order to have the opportunity to respond and interact with these celebrities. In this manner, Twitter facilitates communication with those who were previously inaccessible and provides much needed democratization to the media.

On the other hand, PBS's *Downton Abbey* uses Twitter to bring their protagonists to life. Characters have their own Twitter accounts so that they may tweet their thoughts and continue the conversation with fans long after an episode airs. This clever tactic serves to bolster the connection between the show and its audience and effectively retains viewer interest.

Public Relations and Customer Service

The large presence of customers online warrants using social networks to enhance public relations. Rather than publishing important customer news or policy changes on the company Web site where only a few of even the most loyal customers may see it, companies can now leverage social networks to promote these announcements. Customers appreciate transparency, and efforts by your company to maintain such openness will be recognized.

In addition to providing an additional channel for public relations, social networks also can bolster your customer service platform. American Airlines, for example, has become increasingly sophisticated about providing feedback to troubled customers via Twitter. Besides responding to customer complaints over the phone or by email, American Airlines representatives have been viewing social networks as an additional avenue to serve customers, lending to faster response times because they are able to address multiple customer concerns at once. Their hours of operation on Twitter run from 6 a.m. to midnight CST, reflecting the peak hours that a customer might require support. Expressing an authentic and personable desire to help within each of their conversations, representatives subsequently provide customers with positive, refreshing experiences, setting up the foundations for long-term relationships. By publicly alleviating consumer pains, American Airlines is building customer trust and, in turn, enhancing their brand.[1]

New Media Risks and Control

As organizations become increasingly customer- or constituent-centric through social media campaigns, it is important that they maintain a consistent message throughout. Otherwise, they risk negatively impacting public perception and inadvertently damaging their brand. Celebrities Ashton Kutcher and Kelly Clarkson previously drew criticism from their fans for tweeting their support for controversial public figures whose values appeared misaligned with those of their fans. This inconsistent messaging detrimentally shifted public opinion against Kutcher and Clarkson for a time, forcing the former to temporarily suspend his Twitter account. To avoid this dilemma, organizations must be wary of supporting messages or causes that could create friction with their purported values or they too could alienate customers or constituents.

Controls must be integrated within an organization's social media strategy in order to ensure this alignment. Therefore, it is imperative to set up an infrastructure that will not only pave the way for technological innovation as you improve your positioning among customers, but also establish certain boundaries that cannot be crossed.

United Airlines' failed to set up such an infrastructure within its social media strategy, resulting in a public relations disaster in 2009. After United neglected to respond to customer Dave Carroll after he complained that airline staff had broken his guitar during a recent trip, he turned to online video hub YouTube in order to complain.[2] What resulted was beyond Carroll's and United's expectations, catching the latter especially off guard. Carroll uploaded a video, accompanied by a catchy tune, that featured a humorous re-enactment of United breaking his guitar. The video went viral across the Internet shortly thereafter, and United was forced to address the video publicly. United's lack of infrastructure and subsequent uncertainty over its initial responses via Twitter failed to satisfy Carroll and his own Twitter followers. United Airlines subsequently became the focus of a very public joke, without the online credibility to dissipate the resulting negative perception. Had it set up controls and an infrastructure on how to respond online to such complaints prior to this incident, it could have avoided much embarrassment by one of its very own customers.

References

1. Booth, D. 2012. How American Airlines gets social media right. CNBC.com, July 17.
2. Negroni, C. 2012. With video, a traveler fights back. *The New York Times*, October 28.

Appendix D: Leveraging Mobile Technology for Business Strategy

When you realize that, according to some known predictions, the number of mobile devices will be higher than the number of people living on Earth in 2013, you will understand why you should take mobile into account within your business strategy—often as a complement to your social media strategy as witnessed by Facebook's move into the mobile world itself.

This is to say that while social networks have proven to be excellent tools for information sharing and/or brand awareness, it would not be enough to stop there. Instead, you should look at social networks as only one of the first bricks of your communication strategy—to be completed by other channels, especially the mobile channel.

Just to mention one rather known example of why social networks alone would be insufficient, let us briefly review what happened with vitaminwater's* experience as related by Jed Alpert in his book *The Mobile Marketing Revolution*.[1]

According to Alpert, back in 2009, vitaminwater decided to close down its website to open, instead, a page on Facebook, as many enthusiastic businesses were doing at the peak of the social network's initial phenomenon.

Then, vitaminwater next organized a contest in which thousands of people could participate. Though at a rather high cost, the contest had more than 900,000 participants, out of which the new vitaminwater Connect flavor was born. However, once the contest was over, participants departed from the Facbook page; and there was no longer a chance for vitaminwater to capitalize on this opportunity to maintain a one-on-one dialogue with all of these potential customers.

The lesson learned from this story is that while your organization can use social networks, these social networks alone should not be the sole communication channel utilized by your modern business. This will likely require you to think of leveraging the new form of one-on-one mobile communication, as the number of business opportunities opened by this new mobile world is limitless.

To this effect, just imagine a group of people walking in a shopping mall on a Saturday morning. With mobile devices in hand, some of these people would expect not only to find out if there was a sale going on in the mall, but also to be able to make a just-in-time mortgage payment to their account. At the same time, one of these people also may want to be able to make a money transfer to her teen-age daughter's bank account for her pocket expenses while another may want to be able to pay for a subscription to a new digital outlet—and so forth and so on.

As a business executive or IT leader in today's world economic order, you would surely want to take advantage of this new communication channel to help bring your organization to the next level in terms of meeting customer needs and increasing your market share.

For example, mobile technology has helped Chase Bank bolster its customer service and thereby enhance its brand. In the event that a customer's credit card is fraudulently used, Chase Bank has developed technology to rapidly detect this possible infraction and alert its customers via mobile communication. The responsiveness and effectiveness of Chase's security-related technology differentiate Chase from its competitors and thereby engender in its client base a deeper trust in Chase's overall systems and procedures, increasing the likelihood that customers will use the bank's other products. The knock-on effect created through the implementation of mobile technology such as in this example can, in turn, have a meaningful impact on an organization's ability to increase market share.

While not as exciting as winning market share, the savings that can be made by using this new communication channel also can be very significant. As witness to this statement, let us look at the remarkable savings that Air Canada was reportedly able to achieve with its new self-check-in—up to 80% of the cost of a full service, using mobile technology. Like Air Canada, American Airline recently also got onto the mobile bandwagon by coming up with a series of new mobile applications not only for flight status notification, but also for boarding passes, just to mention a few.

All in all, and as reported in the second case study, try not to pigeonhole your thinking in any existing or legacy technology, but let your imagination go. Let your imagination be driven by the needs of your new strategy, which should dictate to you what kinds of innovative technological solutions you should come up with in order to better serve your customers and increase your business opportunities.

Reference

1. Alpert, J. 2012. *The mobile marketing revolution.* New York: McGraw-Hill.

Appendix E: Leveraging Cloud Computing for Business Strategy

The catchall phrase "the cloud" can be so amorphous and wide-ranging that it is a common source of confusion, but in reality, it is quite simple. The cloud represents products and services managed by a third-party company and made available through the Internet.

In a nutshell, you can access your products and services from anywhere with the cloud. There are few or no switching costs between competing products and services, and there is typically no upfront investment for a cloud product and service.

Before we talk about how an organization could leverage cloud computing for business benefits, let us review cloud computing characteristics—first, in terms of types of cloud, and then in terms of types of services to be rendered over the cloud.

Types of Cloud Computing

Generally speaking, there are three types of clouds.

1. **Public Clouds:** These provide IT applications or activities as a service via the Internet. This type of cloud is called *public* or *external* cloud.
2. **Private Clouds:** These provide IT applications or activities as a service via the organization's Intranet. This type of cloud is called *private* or *internal* cloud, and is built mainly for users internal to an organization.
3. **Hybrid Clouds:** These provide IT applications or activities as a service via public and private clouds.

Types of Cloud Services

While the list below is not intended to be exhaustive, it provides you with a good list of services that can be delivered via the cloud.

1. **Business applications:** This is the same type of transactional applications that we had mentioned previously as part of our discussion on enterprise IT applications architecture.
2. **Collaborative applications:** Included in this category are all of the organization's needs in terms of Web tools, video-conferencing, and audio.
3. **Analytics applications:** Included in this category are all of the applications that have to do with data warehousing and data analytics.
4. **Desktop:** Included in this category are all of the organization's needs in terms of desktop support.
5. **Infrastructure:** Included in this category are all of the organization's needs in terms of servers, archiving, storage, LAN (local area network), and WAN (wide area network) capability.

Benefits and Concerns about Cloud Computing

In a nutshell, below is a summary of cloud computing benefits and concerns:

Benefits

Cloud computing produces a number of advantages:

- You can access products and services stored in the cloud from anywhere.
- You have no switching costs between competing products and services as long as there is data portability.
- There is little to no upfront investment, which means little to no risk.

Common products and services found in the cloud include:

- Hosting for your website(s) or application(s)
- Collaboration tools
- CRM (Customer Relationship Management)

Remember when these were products and services you had to either build in-house or expensively outsource to another company, thereby squandering both money and time? With the cloud, this is no longer the case.

While you are essentially outsourcing these products and services to another company, there is a significant difference with the cloud. Indeed, it has become such a common model that getting one of these aforementioned products and services is as simple as going to a website, entering your credit card information (which will then be charged monthly—no five-year commitments here), and selecting which features you want.

Concerns

The major concern attached to the cloud is that it may not be secure and that your data could be put at risk. While this is a valid concern, reputable cloud product and service providers have put in place more security mechanisms and protocols to ensure the lowest risk possible to your business. Because organizations' businesses depend on the quality of these services, it is in providers' best interests to make sure your organization's data will be safe and secure.

Considerations for Cloud Computing Adoption

While cloud computing offers some distinctively unique advantages, you should carefully evaluate its benefits as part of your overall business strategy and IT roadmap, which should include:

1. Identifying the types of applications and services to be delivered via the cloud.
2. Identifying the types of cloud computing you will need.
3. Identifying the return on investment. In the same way that we have recommended to top executives to take into account their organization's business strategy in prioritizing their IT projects, we will recommend that the same evaluation be done to assess the return of investment (ROI) for cloud computing. By combining all of the users' and customers' needs, you will be able to identify the ROI of cloud computing and, thereafter, determine when and how much you should invest in cloud computing and when to expect to see initial ROI.
4. Identifying the architecture needed for your cloud. Once you have looked at the overall picture of your organization's needs, below are some of the questions you would want to ask yourself and your teams, in order to determine what type of cloud architecture your organization will need:
   a. What services are you going to deliver? To whom and at what frequency?
   b. How are you going to deliver these services?
   c. How will the users access these services?
   d. What type of security needs would the users have for these services?

Appendix F: The Business Case for a New Business Technology Project

The goal of this section is to show the reader how to deal with and integrate a new technology project into the overall IT roadmap formulation process framework.

With the creation of an IT roadmap based on an organization's business strategy, there no longer should be a need to go through the traditional business cases that have been plaguing companies for years. We say plaguing because it is time-consuming, ineffective, and a source of frustration between the business and IT.

This said, in the middle of an IT roadmap execution or even after its completion, there may sometimes be exceptional instances where the company sees an opportunity for a potential business technology project that could generate more revenue or drive considerable cost savings.

In order to help you and your companies know how to deal with these situations, we have devised a review process, as shown in Figure F.1.

By reading Figure F.1, you can see that a business case always starts with one of the business units making a request for the IT department to work on a technology development project for some of the unit's business needs.

From there, if the project budget is lower than a certain amount (which is dependent on the individual company), then the request will be sent to that business unit's IT Steering Committee for evaluation.

If the requested budget is over that amount (say $250,000, in this case), then the Business and IT Governance Board, presided over by the CEO, will be reviewing the business case.

If the business case is rejected, due to a lack of a serious business justification by either the IT Steering Committee or the Business and IT Governance Board, then it will be sent back to that business unit for revision. Otherwise, the business case that the CEO and the Board of Directors just approved will be sent on to the

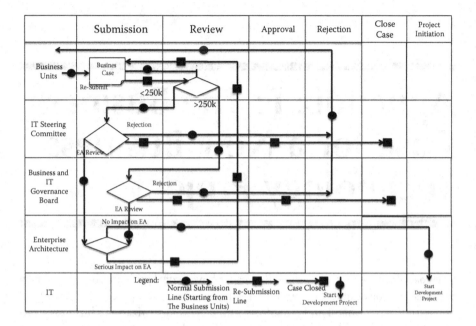

Figure F.1 Review process for a new business case for an IT project.

enterprise architecture (EA) team to evaluate whether there would be any impact on the overall EA, in support of the business strategy.

If it is determined that there would be no serious alteration to the EA, then the EA team will usually give its approval to the IT department, which would then prepare to begin development work, unless there is contention regarding the budget amount.

On the other hand, if the EA team finds that implementing the new project's architecture may have a serious impact on the overall EA, then it will send back the business case to the business unit to refine and resubmit.

When the business case is resubmitted, it will either be approved or else closed if there is a lack of good business justification or if its architectural implementation may negatively impact the company's new business strategy by altering its EA.

Appendix G: Buy or Build (Commercial Off-the-Shelf Package Implementation or In-House Software Development)?

For as long as we can remember, organizations have grappled with the issue of buying versus building. In our context, this remains something to consider because, despite the renewal in in-house software development using Lean and Agile, there still remains the question of whether you should buy or you should build, due precisely to the lack of success companies have had in deploying Agile on a large scale to the entire IT department.

Even though two of us are authors of published books on Agile project management, such as *Business-Driven IT-Wide Implementation of Agile (Scrum) and Kanban (Lean)*,[1] our belief as of today is that, whenever you can, you should buy rather than build. However, this all depends on your situation and the organizational context.

If we could offer some kind of guideline as to when to buy and when to build, then Figure G.1 is what we would suggest that you keep in mind when deciding which course of action you should take—knowing that, for us, in-house software development should only be on the margin of commercial-off-the-shelf (COTS) implementation.

But assuming now that your organization wants to implement COTS software, such as SAP or PeopleSoft ERP (Enterprise Resource Planning) packages or Siebel CRM (Customer Relationship Management) or MS Dynamics, we still believe

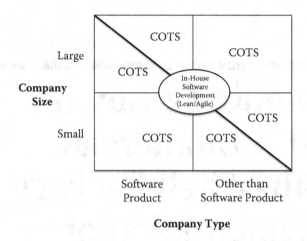

Figure G.1 When to buy and when to build.

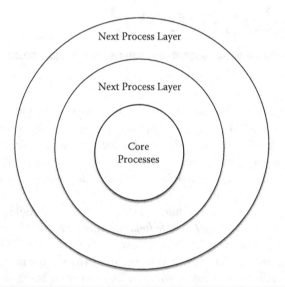

Figure G.2 What ERP or CRM module to implement first?

that using an Agile or incremental approach will be the way to go rather than the traditional big bang process.

The question now is how would we do this? Though every company is different, we can typically do so by identifying the enterprise business processes that relate to the organization's core competency first, then out to the next layer of enterprise business processes (as seen in Figure G.2).

To clarify matters even more, we will suggest, by reading Figure G.2, that you implement the GL (General Ledgers) module first, then AR (Accounts Receivable), then AP (Accounts Payable), then SAP MM (Material Management) if you are a manufacturing company, then SAP SD (Sales and Distribution), and finally Financial Reporting as part of your accounting and financial foundation. Situations will differ from organization to organization, but this is the gist of what we would recommend.

Reference

1. Pham, A., and D. Pham. 2012. *Business-driven IT-wide Agile (Scrum) and Kanban (Lean) implementation: An action guide for business and IT leaders.* New York: Productivity Press.

Glossary

Action Plan: A series of steps that must be carried out in order to successfully execute a strategy. An action plan details specific tasks (such as significant milestones) that will be accomplished, who will be achieving these tasks, and the timeline by which these tasks will be completed.

Application Interface: The way that two software applications are connected using a software program.

Architectural Assessment: An evaluation of software applications, whether they be transactional or BI applications, based on architectural criteria, such as scalability, maintainability, design, and modularity.

Artifact: Any object created by human beings with the intent to be of subsequent use, either as a reference or something that could be improved as part of an effort to enhance it.

B2B: Business to business. A concept that denotes business conducted between companies.

Bargaining Power of Customers: Part of the Five Forces framework, it is the amount of leverage that customers may have over an organization. For example, if one customer can impact the business's volume or affect margins, then this customer holds significant bargaining power.

Bargaining Power of Suppliers: Part of the Five Forces framework, it is the amount of leverage that suppliers may have over an organization. For example, if one supplier can impact the business's volume or affect margins, then this supplier holds significant bargaining power.

Barriers to Entry: Obstacles that prevent new competitors from entering an industry, such as start-up capital requirements or government regulation. Existing companies within an industry may benefit from barriers to entry because such obstacles can prevent new competitors from encroaching upon established market shares.

Batch Interface: As opposed to a real-time interface whereby two software applications dialogue interactively with one another, a batch interface involves data that is sent to a receiving application and is only then picked up sometime later.

Business and IT Governance: The framework of rules and practices by which an organization structures its technology decision-making process in order to ensure alignment of the organization's business strategy with its operations.

Business and IT Strategic Alignment: The process of aligning technology activities and projects with the needs of an organization's business strategy in order to ensure that technology will positively impact the business's bottom line.

Business Model: A set of choices that ultimately describes an organization's logic, from how it operates to the way it creates and captures value, including economic or social value.

Business Process: A set of activities that teams within an organization carry out to accomplish a specific goal.

Business Process Value Modeling: A Lean technique that helps teams streamline processes by distinguishing customer value-added from noncustomer value-added activities.

Cause–Effect Diagram: A diagramming technique, also called the Ishikawa diagramming, which teams can use to identify root causes to a problem, the effects of an action, or the action items they could take to meet a goal.

Cloud: Products and services managed by a third-party company and made available through the Internet.

Competitive Advantage: A sustainable, strategic advantage that an organization possesses over its industry rivals.

Complement: A service or good used in concurrence with another service or good. Though the complementary service or good may possess little value when utilized by itself, it contributes to the offering's overall value when combined with another good or service.

Consistency, Dynamic: A strategy's robust ability to move with a changing, competitive environment and demonstrate continuity. While an organization's value proposition remains similar over time, its delivery of value continues to improve as internal and external conditions alter.

Consistency, External: A strategy's coherence when its external context is considered. The strategy demonstrates alignment with peripheral factors, positively impacting the organization.

Consistency, Internal: The way in which the set of activities that an organization performs meshes in a uniform manner.

Constituents: Internal and external stakeholders within an organization, including employees, suppliers, customers, investors, markets, and society.

Continuous Delivery: One of the 12 Agile principles that places emphasis on delivering software early and frequently to users in order to obtain their feedback as early as possible and make changes or correct errors while it is still not too late or too prohibitive to do so.

Core Competency: A main strength or strategic advantage of a business. Difficult for competitors to replicate, a core competency is the combination of processes, relationships, knowledge, and technical capacities that allow an organization to best serve its customers or constituents.

Customer: The purchaser of a service, product, or idea attained from a supplier or seller.

Database: A physical set of data records.

Data Mart: An analytical database built for and used by a business unit or department to slice and dice for analytical reporting and analysis.

Dynamic Consistency: A strategy's robust ability to move with a changing, competitive environment and demonstrate continuity. While an organization's value proposition remains similar over time, its delivery of value continues to improve as internal and external conditions alter.

EDW (Enterprise Data Warehouse): A clean data store created to merge and store data from different sources for enterprise data analysis.

Enterprise IT Application Architecture: One of the layers of the enterprise architecture (EA) that focuses on the IT application side.

Enterprise Architecture (EA): A process and set of artifacts that can be used to translate an organization's business strategy into an effective IT roadmap, the execution of which should be able to help make that organization's business strategy happen.

Enterprise Architecture (EA) Framework: The way the different layers of the enterprise architecture should fit together.

Enterprise Business Architecture: One of the first layers of the enterprise architecture (EA) that puts the emphasis on the business side as the driving force for everything that follows.

Enterprise IT Data Architecture: One of the layers of the enterprise architecture (EA) that focuses on the IT data architecture side, both for transactional and business intelligence IT data architecture.

Enterprise IT Infrastructure Architecture: One of the enterprise architecture (EA) layers that focuses on the infrastructural needs of an organization.

Enterprise Security Architecture: A new layer of the enterprise architecture (EA) that grows in importance as transactions grow over the Internet.

Entrants, New: Competitors that enter an industry, raising the level of competition. The threat of new entrants depends on the barriers to entry.

External Consistency: A strategy's coherence when its external context is considered. The strategy demonstrates alignment with peripheral factors, positively impacting the organization.

Fit: The consistency between an organization's overall strategy and its core competencies. Also refers to the consistency between an organization's strategy and the choices it makes, given the plausible options and trade-offs.

Five Forces (also see Michael Porter's Five Forces): A framework created by Michael Porter that can be used to analyze the attractiveness of an industry and aid in the development of business strategy. The five forces that make up the framework include analyses of the bargaining power of suppliers, bargaining power of customers, the threat of substitutes, the threat of new entrants, and rivalry among existing competitors.

Fixed Cost: A set expense that does not change, despite a decrease or increase in the amount of services or goods produced. The sum of the fixed costs and variable costs equals the total cost of a service or good.

Flow: Flow is the seamless integration of value-added steps in a business process. Lean experts think they achieve flow when people and materials interact seamlessly and effortlessly. Making operations flow is the ultimate goal of Lean. When waste is reduced and the excess inventory is eliminated, you are left with work that effortlessly flows from start to finish.

Internal Consistency: The way in which the set of activities that an organization performs meshes in a uniform manner.

Industry Structure: The structure of the industry in which a company competes affects its profitability. While otherwise relatively stable, industry structure is ultimately impacted by competing forces, including the bargaining power of suppliers, bargaining power of buyers, threat of substitutes, threat of new entrants, and rivalry among existing competitors.

Ishikawa Diagramming Technique: A diagramming technique that teams can use to identify root causes to a problem, the effects of an action, or the action items they could take to meet a goal.

IT (information technology) Gap: The difference between the current IT situation and artifacts and the future IT situation and artifacts in order to meet the future business needs and strategy.

IT Roadmap: An action plan that matches the organization's business goals with specific technology solutions in order to help meet those goals.

IT Strategy: The overall scope and direction of an IT action plan and organization.

Kaizen: A word in Japanese that indicates a continuous improvement effort.

Lean: A catchphrase that describes a systematic approach to producing more with less, encouraging such systematic thinking through the practice of empowering employees and minimizing waste.

Lean IT Roadmap: An IT action plan and strategy that leverages Lean values and principles.

Lean Portfolio Management: A new approach to managing the portfolio of initiatives or projects of a commercial company or nonprofit association, using Agile and Lean concepts.

MDM (Master Data Management): A new trend in IT, Master Data Management is composed of processes and tools that ultimately help an organization define and manage its master data.

Michael Porter's Five Forces: A framework used to analyze the attractiveness of an industry and aid in the development of business strategy. The five forces that make up the framework include analyses of the bargaining power of suppliers, bargaining power of customers, the threat of substitutes, the threat of new entrants, and rivalry among existing competitors.

Mission: A statement of purpose for an organization.

ODS (Operational Data Store): A data store that integrates data from a range of sources, which is subsequently merged and cleaned to serve as the foundation for enterprise operational reporting. It is an important piece of an Enterprise Data Warehouse (EDW) used for enterprise analytical reporting.

Perfection: Perfection is achieved when the organization can create customer value, identify the value streams, make the work flow, and when the customers pull the product from the providers' supply chain.

Product–Market Growth Directions Matrix: Originally developed by applied mathematician Igor Ansoff, the matrix captures an organization's current position in the market and its potential opportunities for growth, based on various combinations of markets and products.

Profit Margin: A measurement that represents how much of each dollar in revenue an organization actually retains in earnings.

Pull: A Lean principle which considers that a product should be pulled by the customers from the providers' supply chain, rather than being pushed by the providers to the distributors onto the customers.

Pull Organization: A pull organization is one in which the supply chain sends a product through the supply chain because there is a specific demand for that one product, as opposed to creating all the products first as inventory and "pushing" them out to distributors or customers.

Real-Time Interface: As opposed to a batch interface where data sent to the receiving application is picked up only sometime later, a real-time interface is one where two software applications dialogue interactively with one another.

Relative Cost: The cost of an input, such as material or labor, that is used by an organization to produce a final service or product as compared to the cost of that same input when used by another organization.

Rivalry: Competition for the same objective within a given industry. The intensity of rivalry depends on strategic objectives, degree of differentiation, the structure of competition, the structure of industry costs, switching costs, and exit barriers.

Standardization, Product: The process of establishing consistent characteristics for a specific service or good.

Strategic Choice: A decision made by an organization that aligns well with its core competencies and its overall business strategy.

Strategic Option: Prospective actions that an organization can take, in response to the external or internal situation, in light of the various trade-offs and opportunities.

Strategy Blade: The visualization of an organization's system of value creation that is specific to its core competency and strategy.

Strategy, Business: The long-term direction and scope of an organization, intending to achieve particular business goals.

Strategy, Differentiation: An approach whereby an organization develops unique products or services targeted at certain customer or constituent segments, allowing them to compete on nonprice factors. Typically adopted when an organization has clear competitive advantages and can sustain extensive marketing efforts.

Strategy, Evolving: A business strategy that incorporates dynamism, demonstrating an understanding of the external and internal context.

Strategy, Low-Cost: An approach whereby an organization offers a low price relative to rivals in order to incite demand and acquire market share. Typically adopted by a company when its product has few or no competitive advantage or when higher production volumes can lead to economies of scale.

Strategy, Social: An approach whereby a company aims to better engage and interact with its constituents, leveraging online tools, such as social networks.

Substitute: A product or service that can satisfy the same need of a customer as another product or service and, therefore, may be used to replace the latter.

Supplier: A party that provides services or products. May also be referred to as a vendor.

Timeline: A chronological display of events, often used to establish goals and milestones as part of an action plan.

TOGAF: A well-known enterprise architecture (EA) framework by the Open Group.

TPS (Toyota Production System): Invented by Ochii Ohno, it is considered to be the engine behind the revival and growth of the Japanese auto industry after World War II.

Trade-Off: The foregoing of an attractive outcome in exchange for attaining (or at least, increasing the likelihood of) another attractive outcome, in order to maximize effectiveness or return given the present circumstances.

Value: The main idea here is for providers to maximize the customer value of a product or service, as defined by the customers.

Value Chain: The set of both primary and support activities or processes that an organization sets up to perform in order to achieve its mission and goals.

Value Creation: Actions by an organization that serve to enhance the worth of the organization's offering, if not the organization's overall business from a social or economic standpoint.

Value Proposition: The promise of value to be delivered by an organization. Typically addresses which customer needs the organization will meet and how it will price its offerings.

Value Stream: A value stream is a set of actions needed to bring a product to an organization's customers.

Variable Cost: Expenses that change in proportion to business activity, e.g., increasing as production increases. The variable cost aggregates the marginal costs over all units produced. The sum of the fixed costs and variable costs equals the total cost of a service or good.

Virtualization: The process of creating a virtual version of a resource, such as an operating system, hardware platform, or storage device.

Vision: An aspirational description of the achievements an organization aims to accomplish in the mid-to-long term.

Willingness to Pay (WTP): The maximum price that a customer or constituent is willing to pay in order to purchase a service or good.

Zachman Framework™, The: An enterprise architecture (EA) framework by John A. Zachman.

Index

Printed in the United States
by Baker & Taylor Publisher Services